First World War
and Army of Occupation
War Diary
France, Belgium and Germany

16 DIVISION
47 Infantry Brigade
Royal Irish Regiment
6th Battalion
17 December 1915 - 9 February 1918

WO95/1970/3

The Naval & Military Press Ltd
www.nmarchive.com
Published in association with The National Archives

Published by

The Naval & Military Press Ltd

Unit 10 Ridgewood Industrial Park,

Uckfield, East Sussex,

TN22 5QE England

Tel: +44 (0) 1825 749494

www.naval-military-press.com

www.nmarchive.com

This diary has been reprinted in facsimile from the original. Any imperfections are inevitably reproduced and the quality may fall short of modern type and cartographic standards.

© Crown Copyright
Images reproduced by permission of The National Archives, London, England, 2015.

Contents

Document type	Place/Title	Date From	Date To
Heading	WO95/1970 16 Div-47 Inf Bde 6 Royal Irish Regt Dec 1915-Feb 1918		
Heading	16th Division 47th Infy Bde 6th Bn Roy. Irish Regt Dec 1915-Feb 1918 Disbanded Feb 1918		
Heading	47/16th Div 6th R. Inf Rgt Vol I Dec 15 Feb 18 6th R. Inf Regt. Vol I		
War Diary	Blackdown	17/12/1915	17/12/1915
War Diary	Southampton	17/12/1915	17/12/1915
War Diary	Havre	18/12/1915	18/12/1915
War Diary	Choques (36A V 29)	19/12/1915	19/12/1915
War Diary	Drouvin (36B K4)	19/12/1915	19/12/1915
War Diary	Drouvin	19/12/1915	30/12/1915
War Diary	Ameptes (36B B3)	30/12/1915	31/12/1915
War Diary	Bomy	31/12/1915	31/12/1915
Heading	6th R. Irish Rgt. Vol. 2		
War Diary	Bomy	01/01/1916	04/01/1916
War Diary	Matringhem	05/01/1916	08/01/1916
War Diary	Febvin Palfart	09/01/1916	12/01/1916
War Diary	Allouagne	13/01/1916	13/01/1916
War Diary	Verquin	14/01/1916	14/01/1916
War Diary	Phildsophe	15/01/1916	26/01/1916
War Diary	Noeux-Les Mines	26/01/1916	27/01/1916
War Diary	Hesdigneul	27/01/1916	27/01/1916
War Diary	Febvin Palfart	28/01/1916	29/01/1916
Heading	6th R. Irish Rgt. Vol. 3.		
War Diary	Febvin Palfart	01/02/1916	06/02/1916
War Diary	Bellerive	07/02/1916	07/02/1916
War Diary	Essars	08/02/1916	14/02/1916
War Diary	Festubert	14/02/1916	16/02/1916
War Diary	Essars	17/02/1916	17/02/1916
War Diary	Busnettes	18/02/1916	18/02/1916
War Diary	Bellery	19/02/1916	19/02/1916
War Diary	Beaumetz Les Aire	20/02/1916	29/02/1916
Heading	6 ? Reg Vol 4		
War Diary	Cottes	01/03/1916	08/03/1916
War Diary	Allouagne Annequin	11/03/1916	14/03/1916
War Diary	Burbure	17/03/1916	25/03/1916
War Diary	Noeux-Les-Mines	25/08/1916	25/08/1916
War Diary	Loos (G 36. Sheet 36 C)	25/03/1916	26/03/1916
War Diary	Loos	27/03/1916	29/03/1916
War Diary	Philosophe	30/03/1916	31/03/1916
War Diary	Mazingarbe	01/04/1916	06/04/1916
War Diary	Trenches Before Hulloch	06/04/1916	16/04/1916
War Diary	Philosophe	20/04/1916	20/04/1916
War Diary	Noeux-Les-Mines	24/04/1916	29/04/1916
War Diary	Loos	30/04/1916	03/05/1916
War Diary	Support Trenches	03/05/1916	07/05/1916
Heading	To DAG 3rd Echelon Base Herewith War Diary of my Battalion for May 1916	01/06/1916	01/06/1916
War Diary	Loos	08/05/1916	12/05/1916

War Diary	Support Trenches	16/05/1916	16/05/1916
War Diary	Mazingarbe	17/05/1916	25/05/1916
War Diary	Trenches N Of Loos	26/05/1916	31/05/1916
Miscellaneous	To Officer incharge Adjutant Generals office Base	01/07/1916	01/07/1916
War Diary	Trenches Near Puits 14 Bis	01/06/1916	06/06/1916
War Diary	Philosophe	07/06/1916	10/06/1916
War Diary	Noeux-Les-Mines	11/06/1916	17/06/1916
War Diary	Loos	17/06/1916	21/06/1916
War Diary	Philosophe	24/06/1916	24/06/1916
War Diary	Loos	24/06/1916	29/06/1916
War Diary	Philosophe	30/06/1916	30/06/1916
Heading	War Diary 6th (f) Bn The Royal Irish Rgt 1st July To 31st. July 1916 Volume No. 8		
War Diary	Philosophe	01/07/1916	03/07/1916
War Diary	Mazingarbe	03/07/1916	11/07/1916
War Diary	Trenches Near Puits 14 Bis.	12/07/1916	14/07/1916
War Diary	Trenches Near Puits 14 Bis	15/07/1916	31/07/1916
War Diary	Noeux-Les Mines	31/07/1916	31/07/1916
Heading	War Diary 6th Royal Irish Regiment Month Of August 1916 Volume 9		
War Diary	Noeux-Les-Mines	01/08/1916	09/08/1916
War Diary	Loos	09/08/1916	24/08/1916
War Diary	Noeux-Les-Mines	24/08/1916	25/08/1916
War Diary	Burbure	26/08/1916	28/08/1916
War Diary	Sand-Pit Mr Meaulte	29/08/1916	30/08/1916
War Diary	Carnoy	30/08/1916	31/08/1916
War Diary	Sand-Pit Meaulte		
War Diary	Carnoy		
Heading	War Diary 6th Royal Irish Regiment Month Of September 1916 Volume 10		
War Diary	Carnoy	01/09/1916	03/09/1916
War Diary	Guillemont	03/09/1916	03/09/1916
War Diary	Carnoy	04/09/1916	04/09/1916
War Diary	Sunken Road	07/09/1916	10/09/1916
War Diary	Carnoy	10/09/1916	12/09/1916
War Diary	Vaux	14/09/1916	17/09/1916
War Diary	Huppy	18/09/1916	24/09/1916
War Diary	M.6.D. 6.7.	25/09/1916	30/09/1916
Heading	War Diary Month Of October, 1916. Volume 11 6th Royal Irish Regiment.		
War Diary	Laclytte	01/10/1916	01/10/1916
War Diary	Siege Fm	05/10/1916	06/10/1916
War Diary	York House	09/10/1916	12/10/1916
War Diary	Butterfly Fm	13/10/1916	19/10/1916
War Diary	Siege Fm	21/10/1916	21/10/1916
War Diary	York House	25/10/1916	27/10/1916
War Diary	M 6 D Laclytte	29/10/1916	31/10/1916
Heading	War Diary For Month Of November 1916 Volume 12 6th R. Irish Regiment.		
War Diary	Curraghcamp	01/11/1916	04/11/1916
War Diary	Siege Fm	06/11/1916	09/11/1916
War Diary	York House	10/11/1916	14/11/1916
War Diary	Butterfly Fm	15/11/1916	22/11/1916
War Diary	Siege Fm	24/11/1916	25/11/1916
War Diary	York House	26/11/1916	30/11/1916

Heading	War Diary For Month Of December, 1916 Volume 13. 6th R Irish Regiment. Vol. 13		
War Diary	Currach Camp	01/12/1916	11/12/1916
War Diary	Cooker Farm	12/12/1916	20/12/1916
War Diary	Derry Huts	24/12/1916	28/12/1916
War Diary	Cooker Farm	29/12/1916	31/12/1916
Heading	War Diary For Month Of January, 1917 Volume 14 6th Royal Irish Regiment.		
War Diary	Cooker Farm	01/01/1917	05/01/1917
War Diary	Curragh Camp	07/01/1917	13/01/1917
War Diary	Cooker Farm	15/01/1917	21/01/1917
War Diary	Derry Huts	26/01/1917	26/01/1917
War Diary	Cooker Farm	27/01/1917	29/01/1917
War Diary	Derry Huts	30/01/1917	31/01/1917
Heading	War Diary For Month Of February 1917 Volume 15 6th Royal Irish Regiment. Vol 15		
War Diary	Derry Huts	01/01/1917	02/01/1917
War Diary	Foat Victoria	03/01/1917	08/01/1917
War Diary	Doncaster Huts	07/02/1916	17/02/1916
War Diary	F T Victoria	18/01/1917	22/01/1917
War Diary	Ncasterh	24/01/1917	27/01/1917
Heading	War Diary For Month Of March, 1917 Volume 16 6th Btn Royal Irish Regiment Vol 16		
War Diary	Doncaster Huts	01/03/1917	01/03/1917
War Diary	Ft Victoria	02/03/1917	05/03/1917
War Diary	Derry Huts	06/03/1917	09/03/1917
War Diary	Ft Victoria	10/03/1917	13/03/1917
War Diary	Doctor's House	13/03/1917	14/03/1917
War Diary	Erthen	14/03/1917	19/03/1917
War Diary	Berthen Area	20/03/1917	31/03/1917
Heading	War Diary For Month Of April, 1917. Volume 17 6th R. Irish Regiment.		
War Diary	Kemmel Shelters Right Subsection Wytschaete Sector.	01/04/1917	01/04/1917
War Diary	Right Subsection Wytschaete Section	02/04/1917	05/04/1917
War Diary	Butterfly Farm	05/04/1917	10/04/1917
War Diary	Right Subsection Wytschaete	11/04/1917	15/04/1917
War Diary	Rossignol Estaminet	16/04/1917	19/04/1917
War Diary	Kemmel Shelters	20/04/1917	24/04/1917
War Diary	Clare Camp	25/04/1917	30/04/1917
Heading	War Diary Volume 18 For Month Of May, 1917 6th R Irish Regiment. Vol 18		
War Diary	Clare Camp	01/05/1917	05/05/1917
War Diary	Right Subsection Wytschaete	06/05/1917	09/05/1917
War Diary	Carnarvon Camp St Sylvestre Cappel	10/05/1917	15/05/1917
War Diary	Ebblinghem Wizerves.	16/05/1917	17/05/1917
War Diary	Alquines	18/05/1917	28/05/1917
War Diary	Wizernes	29/05/1917	29/05/1917
War Diary	Staples	30/05/1917	30/05/1917
War Diary	Clare Camp	31/05/1917	31/05/1917
Heading	War Diary. For Month Of June, 1917. Volume 19 6th Btn Royal Irish Regiment Vol 19		
War Diary	Clare Camp	01/06/1917	01/06/1917
War Diary	Renmore Line	02/06/1917	06/06/1917
War Diary	Nap Support	07/06/1917	07/06/1917
War Diary	Petit Bois	07/06/1917	07/06/1917
War Diary	Rossignol Wood	08/06/1917	08/06/1917

War Diary	Renmore Camp	09/06/1917	13/06/1917
War Diary	Merris Area	13/06/1917	18/06/1917
War Diary	Eecke	19/06/1917	20/06/1917
War Diary	Bollezeele	21/06/1917	30/06/1917
Heading	War Diary For Month Of July, 1917. Volume 20 6th R Irish Regiment.		
War Diary	Bollezeele Area	01/07/1917	15/07/1917
War Diary	Tilques Training Area	16/07/1917	23/07/1917
War Diary	Winnizeele No. 2. Area	25/07/1917	25/07/1917
War Diary	Watou No. 3 Area	26/07/1917	31/07/1917
War Diary	War Diary. For Month Of August, 1917, Volume 21 6th Royal Irish Regt.		
War Diary	Brandhoek Area No. 1	01/08/1917	01/08/1917
War Diary	Up The Line	02/08/1917	02/08/1917
War Diary	Front Line	03/08/1917	05/08/1917
War Diary	Brandhoek No. 2 Area Toronto Camp.	06/08/1917	10/08/1917
War Diary	Square Farm Front Line	11/08/1917	15/08/1917
War Diary	Vlamertinghe No. 3. Area Bivouac Camp.	16/08/1917	16/08/1917
War Diary	Eitel Fritz Trench (Supports)	17/08/1917	17/08/1917
War Diary	Vlamertinghe No. 3 Area	18/08/1917	18/08/1917
War Diary	Watou (B) Area.	19/08/1917	19/08/1917
War Diary	Eecke Area	20/08/1917	21/08/1917
War Diary	By Train to Bapaume	22/08/1917	22/08/1917
War Diary	Camp near Gomiecourt And Achiet Le Grand	23/08/1917	25/08/1917
War Diary	Ervillers	25/08/1917	25/08/1917
War Diary	Bullecourt Line	26/08/1917	31/08/1917
Heading	War Diary. For Month Of 1917, Volume 22 6th Royal Irish Regiment. Vol 22		
War Diary	Line W. Of Bullecourt	01/09/1917	03/09/1917
War Diary	Camp near Ervillers	04/09/1917	14/09/1917
War Diary	Line West Of Bullecourt	15/09/1917	23/09/1917
War Diary	In Support. Rly Reserve.	24/09/1917	30/09/1917
Heading	War Diary For Month Of October, 1917. 6th Royal Irish Regiment. Volume Number 23		
War Diary	Bullecourt Line & Ervillers	01/10/1917	15/10/1917
War Diary	Ervillers	16/10/1917	16/10/1917
War Diary	Bullecourt Line	17/10/1917	31/10/1917
Heading	War Diary For Month Of November, 1917. Volume. 24 6th R. Irish Regiment		
War Diary	Line N. Of Bullecourt	01/11/1917	02/11/1917
War Diary	Durrow Camp	03/11/1917	12/11/1917
War Diary	Line N. Of Bullecourt. Left Sub Section	13/11/1917	18/11/1917
War Diary	Durrow Camp	19/11/1917	21/11/1917
War Diary	Line. Left. Subs Section N. Of Bullecourt	22/11/1917	30/11/1917
Heading	War Diary. For Month Of December. 1917 Volume 25 6th R. Irish Regiment.		
War Diary	Trenches N.W. Of Bullecourt (Tunnel TR.)	01/12/1917	02/12/1917
War Diary	On The March	03/12/1917	03/12/1917
War Diary	Beaulencourt	04/12/1917	05/12/1917
War Diary	On The March Buire	07/12/1917	11/12/1917
War Diary	Ste Emilie	12/12/1917	14/12/1917
War Diary	Epehy Sector Right Sub Section	17/12/1917	21/12/1917
War Diary	Epeay Sector Right Sub Section	22/12/1917	23/12/1917
War Diary	Villers Faucon	24/12/1917	28/12/1917
War Diary	Left Section Epehy Section	29/12/1917	31/12/1917

Heading	War Diary For Month Of January. 1918. Volume 26 6th R. Irish Regiment.		
War Diary	Epehy Sector Left Section	01/01/1918	10/01/1918
War Diary	Tincourt Dwint Reserve	11/01/1918	21/01/1918
War Diary	Epehy Sector Right Section	22/01/1918	31/01/1918
Heading	War Diary. For Month Of February, 1918 Volume 24. 6th Royal Irish Regiment.		
War Diary		01/02/1918	01/02/1918
War Diary	Lempire	02/02/1918	02/02/1918
War Diary	Saulcourt	03/02/1918	09/02/1918

WO 95/1970

16 Div - 49 Inf Bde

6 Royal Irish Regt

Dec 1915 - Feb 1918

16TH DIVISION
47TH INFY BDE

6TH BN ROY. IRISH REGT
DEC 1915-FEB 1918

DISBANDED FEB 1918

6th R. Ir. Rgt.
Vol I

121/7910

Dec 15
Feb '18

Original
Confidential

December 1915.

Army Form C. 2118.

WAR DIARY or INTELLIGENCE SUMMARY

of 6th (S) Bn The Royal Irish Regt.

(Erase heading not required.)

Instructions regarding War Diaries and Intelligence Summaries are contained in F.S. Regs., Part II. and the Staff Manual respectively. Title pages will be prepared in manuscript.

Place	Date	Hour	Summary of Events and Information	Remarks and references to Appendices
BLACKDOWN	17.12.15	4 p.m.	The Battalion left BLACKDOWN to join the British Expeditionary Force in FRANCE. It formed part of the 47th Infantry Brigade of the 16th (Irish) Division, and was commanded by Lt. Colonel F.E.P. Curzon.	
SOUTHAMPTON	"	8 p.m.	Arrived at SOUTHAMPTON	
	"	4.30 p.m.	Left SOUTHAMPTON 27 officers and 826 men on board S.S. LA MARGUERITE. 6 " 170 " with the Regt Transport on board S.S. BELLEROPHON	
HAVRE	18.12.15	8 a.m.	Disembarked at HAVRE and marched to a Regt Camp there.	
		9.15 p.m.	Left HAVRE by train	
CHOQUES (36 A V 29)	19.12.15	6 p.m.	Arrived at CHOQUES and disentrained.	
		7.30 p.m.	Left CHOQUES on foot for DROUVIN	
DROUVIN (36 B K 4)	19.12.15	9.15 p.m.	Arrived at DROUVIN and went into billets there.	
	22.12.15		The Battalion was attached to the 4th Army Corps in the 1st Army and was attached to the 47th Division for instruction in Trench Warfare.	
	23.12.15		C.O., Adjt, two other officers and 25 other ranks were attached to the 8th London Regt (Post Office Rifles) from 23-12-15 — 25-12-15 and spent this time in the front line trenches in front of VERMELLES, and immediately to the HULLUCH road (Map 36 C.G 12 d)	

Original
December 1915 Confidential

WAR DIARY
of
INTELLIGENCE SUMMARY.

6th (S) Bn The Royal Irish Regt.

Army Form C. 2118.

Place	Date	Hour	Summary of Events and Information	Remarks and references to Appendices
DROUVIN	25.12.15		A scout party of 3 Officers & 22 O.R. Spent 48 hours in front line trenches held 25-12-15 and 27-12-15. This party was also attached to the 8th London Regt.	
	27.12.15	5 pm	A working party of 300 Officers and men went into the Reserve Trenches East of VERMELLES (36c G8) to improve the Trenches there. Party returned about midnight.	
	30.12.15	6.30 am	Left DROUVIN to march to BOMY	
AMETTES (36 B B3)		3.30 pm	Arrived at AMETTES and billeted there for the night.	
	31.12.15	8.30 am	Left AMETTES.	
BOMY		12 noon	Arrived at BOMY (Belgian Sq C6) and billeted there.	
	1-1-16			

Lindsay Burgoyne Lt Colonel
(Ldg Comdg) 6th Royal Irish Regt

2 f.

6th R. Inst Rgt.
vol: 2

16"

47/16

Original

Confidential

Army Form C. 2118.

WAR DIARY

of 6th (S) Bn
The Royal Irish Regt
January 1916

INTELLIGENCE SUMMARY.

(Erase heading not required.)

Instructions regarding War Diaries and Intelligence Summaries are contained in F.S. Regs., Part II. and the Staff Manual respectively. Title pages will be prepared in manuscript.

Place	Date	Hour	Summary of Events and Information	Remarks and references to Appendices
BOMY	1-1-16		On this date the Battalion was still billeted at BOMY (Map Reference BELGIUM HAZEBROUCK 5A C 6)	Ath.
BOMY	4-1-16	11:30am	left BOMY and marched to MATRINGHEM (Sheet 5A B 6)	Ath.
MATRINGHEM	5-1-16	2 pm	Inspected by Lieut Gen Sir H. WILSON Comdg 4th Corps.	Ath.
MATRINGHEM	8-1-16	12:30 pm	left MATRINGHEM and marched to FEBVIN-PALFART (Sheet 5A D 6)	Ath.
FEBVIN PALFART	9-1-16		Commenced a course of training in musketry and Bombing.	Ath.
FEBVIN PALFART	12-1-16	12:30 pm	left FEBVIN-PALFART and marched to ALLOUAGNE (Sheet 5A G 6)	Ath.
ALLOUAGNE	13-1-16	12:30 pm	left ALLOUAGNE and marched to VERQUIN (Sheet 5A H 6)	Ath.
VERQUIN	14-1-16		From this date the Battalion was attached for instruction to the 44th Infantry Brigade, 15th (Scottish) Division. Marched to PHILOSOPHE (FRANCE Sheet 36C G 20 C) and were billeted here for the night.	Ath.

Original

Confidential

Army Form C. 2118.

Instructions regarding War Diaries and Intelligence Summaries are contained in F. S. Regs, Part II. and the Staff Manual respectively. Title pages will be prepared in manuscript.

WAR DIARY of 6th (S) Bn. The Royal Irish Regt

INTELLIGENCE SUMMARY.
(Erase heading not required.)

January 1916

Place	Date	Hour	Summary of Events and Information	Remarks and references to Appendices
PHILOSOPHE	15-1-16		Battalion Head Quarters remained at PHILOSOPHE. Each Company of the Battalion was attached to a Battalion of the 44th Infantry Brigade already in the trenches, occupying the front of the line N.E. of LOOS from H.19.A.1.8 to G.36.D.4.2 Sheet 36C FRANCE Companies joined their Battalions as under.	✓
	15.1.16	5 p.m.	A Coy. left PHILOSOPHE to join 9th BLACK WATCH	
		5.30 p.m.	2 platoons B Coy. left to join 10th GORDON HIGHLANDERS.	
		6 p.m.	Machine Gun Section with 4 Lewis machine Guns moved up to take over a portion of this line.	✓
PHILOSOPHE	16.1.16	5 p.m.	C Coy. left to join 7th CAMERON HIGHLANDERS	✓
		5.30 p.m.	D Coy. left to join 8th SEAFORTH HIGHLANDERS	
		6 p.m.	2 platoons B Coy. left to join 10th GORDON HIGHLANDERS.	
PHILOSOPHE	16.1.16		3 NCOs then wounded, in trenches.	✓
	17-1-16		1 man Killed, 1 wounded.	✓
	18-1-16		1 man wounded	✓
	19.1.16		1 man wounded	✓

Original
Confidential   3

Army Form C. 2118.

Instructions regarding War Diaries and Intelligence
Summaries are contained in F.S. Regs., Part II.
and the Staff Manual respectively. Title pages
will be prepared in manuscript.

WAR DIARY of 6th (S) Bn The Royal Irish Regt

INTELLIGENCE SUMMARY.

(Erase heading not required.)

January 1916.

Place	Date	Hour	Summary of Events and Information	Remarks and references to Appendices
PHILOSOPHE	21-1-16		2 men killed, one man wounded in trenches.	W.D.
	23-1-16		1 man wounded.	W.D.
	24-1-16		4 men wounded.	W.D.
	25-1-16		1 O.R. wounded	W.D.
	26-1-16		Major G.W. LE PAGE Officer Commanding D Coy killed, O.R. 1 killed, 3 wounded	W.D.
	26-1-16	3pm	Battalion Headquarters left PHILOSOPHE and moved to NOEUX-LES-MINES (Sheet 36B K.15)	W.D.
NOEUX-LES MINES	26-1-16		During the night 26-1-16 / 27-1-16 the 46th Inf Brigade was relieved by the 46th Inf Brigade. The 4 Companies of the 6th Royal Irish Regt left the trenches with their respective Battalions and joined Bn Headquarters at NOEUX-LES-MINES. The Machine Gun Section remained in the trenches in case an expected attack by the Germans should take place. No important operations took place while the Battalion was in the trenches but various parts of the line were heavily shelled from time to time.	W.D.
NOEUX-LES MINES	27-1-16	1pm	Left NOEUX-LES-MINES and marched to HESDIGNEUL (Sheet 36B E.25)	W.D.
	27-1-16		Casualties in Machine Gun Section O.R. 1 Killed & 2 missing.	W.D.

Original
Confidential

Army Form C. 2118.

Instructions regarding War Diaries and Intelligence Summaries are contained in F. S. Regs., Part II. and the Staff Manual respectively. Title pages will be prepared in manuscript.

WAR DIARY of 6th (S) Bn. The Royal Irish Regt.
INTELLIGENCE SUMMARY
(Erase heading not required.)

January 1916

Place	Date	Hour	Summary of Events and Information	Remarks and references to Appendices
HERBIGNEUL	27-1-16	9.30a	Left HERBIGNEUL and marched via AVCHEL (Sheet 36 C.28) to AMETTES (B4) halted here at 1.30pm for an hour and marched on then to FEBVIN - PALFART (Sheet 36A S.28)	
			On the night of the 27th/28th the Machine Gun Section was relieved and rejoined the unit on the 29-1-16.	
FEBVIN PALFART	28-1-16		The Battalion arrived at their billets in FEBVIN - PALFART at 5.15 pm.	
	29-1-16		A course of training in musketry, Bombing and Drill was continued to the end of the month.	
	1-2-16.			

Stanley Burgoyne
Lieut Colonel
Comdg 6th Royal Irish Regt.

26.

6th R. Irish Rgt.
vol. 3

Confidential
Original
Army Form C. 2118.

WAR DIARY
or
INTELLIGENCE SUMMARY.
(Erase heading not required.)

of 6th (S) Bn
The Royal Irish Regiment   Sheet 1
February 1916

Place	Date	Hour	Summary of Events and Information	Remarks and references to Appendices
FESVIN PALFART	1.2.16		At the opening of the month the Battalion was in Back billets at FESVIN – PALFART (BELGIUM Sq Square D6)	
do	6.2.16	9am	Left FESVIN – PALFART and marched via LILLERS to BELLERIVE (Sheet 36A. V.6) arriving at 4pm.	
BELLERIVE	7.2.16	8.30am	Left BELLERIVE and marched via BETHUNE to ESSARS (Sheet 36A. x.25) arriving at 10.30 am. From this date the Battalion was attached to the 2nd Division under orders of 1st Corps.	
ESSARS	8.2.16		A and B Coys were attached to the 99th Inf Brigade and relieved 2 Companies of the 1st KRRC in the trenches occupied by the 1st KRRC in front of GIVENCHY (Sheet 36.c Sq A9). These two companies were under orders of the O.C. 1st KRRC.	
	9.2.16		C and D Coys were attached to the 5th Inf Brigade and relieved 2 Companies of the 2nd H.L.I. in the trenches occupied by the 2nd H.L.I. East of FESTUBERT at Sheet 36. S.27. Casualties OR. 2 wounded.	
ESSARS	9.2.16		Casualties OR. 1 wounded	
	10.2.16		Casualties OR 8 wounded	
	11.2.16			
ESSARS	12.2.16		A and B Coys were relieved by 2 Companies of the 22nd Royal Fusiliers and returned to ESSARS about 11 pm. Similarly C and D Coys were relieved by 2 Coys of the 1st Herts Regt and returned to ESSARS about 10.30pm	

Original
Army Form C. 2118.
Sheet 2

Confidential

Instructions regarding War Diaries and Intelligence Summaries are contained in F.S. Regs., Part II. and the Staff Manual respectively. Title pages will be prepared in manuscript.

WAR DIARY of the 6th (S) Bn.
The Royal Irish Regt.
February 1916

INTELLIGENCE SUMMARY

(Erase heading not required.)

Place	Date	Hour	Summary of Events and Information	Remarks and references to Appendices
ESSARS	13.2.16		Casualties. 1 O.R. (attached to the 17th Middlesex Regt.) wounded. From this date the Battalion was attached to the 6th Inf. Brigade	
ESSARS	14.2.16	5 pm	Left ESSARS and proceeded to take over the front line trenches then occupied by the 17th Middlesex Regt. in C1 Sub-Section (FESTUBERT). The relief was completed at 9.10 p.m. The line held extended from FIFE ROAD (A.3.c.7.6.) Sheet 36c to S.27.b.4.2. Sheet 36 and was held as follows:— Front line consisted of 16 isolated breastworks known as "Islands" and was held by two half companies (A and D). These were relieved after 24 hours by the other half of their respective companies. Support Line consisted of a continuous breastwork 800 yards in rear of the front line and was occupied by 2½ Companies. Reserve of ½ company was kept in FESTUBERT VILLAGE (Sheet 36 S.25) in the support line. Battalion Headquarters was situated in the support line. The battalion held the right subsection of the line held by the 6th Inf. Brigade and had on its left flank the 1st Herts Regt. On the right was the 99th Inf. Brigade with the 1st Berks Regt. On the left in touch with us.	
FESTUBERT	14.2.16			
	15.2.16		No unusual activity beyond constant sniping took place.	

Confidential

Original

Army Form C. 2118
Sheet 3

WAR DIARY of the 6th (S) Bn The Royal Irish Regt
INTELLIGENCE SUMMARY
February 1916

(Erase heading not required.)

Instructions regarding War Diaries and Intelligence Summaries are contained in F.S. Regs., Part II. and the Staff Manual respectively. Title Pages will be prepared in manuscript.

Place	Date	Hour	Summary of Events and Information	Remarks and references to Appendices
FESTUBERT	16.2.16		Relieved by 2nd South Staff Regt. Relief commenced at 6.30 p.m. and was completed at 8.10 p.m. On relief, the battalion returned to ESSARS. During the period that the Battalion was in the trenches there were no casualties.	
ESSARS	17.2.16	9 a.m.	Left ESSARS and marched via BETHUNE and CHOCQUES to BUSNETTES (Sheet 36A Sq V14d)	
BUSNETTES	18.2.16	9.30 a.m	Left BUSNETTES and marched via LILLERS to BELLERY (Sheet 36B Sq B5a)	
BELLERY	19.2.16	10 a.m.	Left BELLERY and marched to BEAUMETZ-LES-AIRE (BELGIUM Sheet 5A Sq C6)	
BEAUMETZ LES AIRE	20.2.16		Draft of 40 O.R. joined from 3rd Royal Irish Regt.	
	21.2.16		The Battalion was inspected by Lieut General Sir H. GOUGH, Cmdg 1st CORPS. Major H.P.E. Parker transferred to ENGLAND and struck off the strength of the Battalion. 48 O.R. having been found medically unfit by A.D.M.S. 16th Division were transferred to the 16th Infantry Base Depot.	
	25.2.16		The Battalion was inspected by General Sir C. MONRO, Cmdg 1st ARMY.	
	27.2.16	8.15 a.m.	Left BEAUMETZ-LES-AIRE and marched to COTTES (Sheet 36A Sq T.11.) arriving at 1.45 p.m.	

Shipley Burgo Lt Colonel
Comm. ag 6th Royal Irish Regt

7.3.16.

6 Jn Reg

vol 4

Confidential

Signed

Army Form C. 2118
Sheet 1.

WAR DIARY of 6th(S) Bn
or The Royal Sussex Regiment
INTELLIGENCE SUMMARY
March 1916

(Erase heading not required.)

Instructions regarding War Diaries and Intelligence Summaries are contained in F.S. Regs., Part II. and the Staff Manual respectively. Title Pages will be prepared in manuscript.

Place	Date	Hour	Summary of Events and Information	Remarks and references to Appendices
COTTES	1.3.16		At the beginning of the month the Batt'n was in back billets at COTTES T.11 Sheet 36A.	Jh.
	5.3.16		Major GARRAWAY. C.W., 2nd in Command, left the Batt'n on his appointment as Town Major of NOEUX-LES-MINES. A draft of 19 O.R. joined from the 3rd Battalion.	Jh.
	8.3.16	9.15am	Marched to ALLOUAGNE C.12. Sheet 36 B. arriving 12 hoon	Jh. Jh.
ALLOUAGNE	11.3.16	9am.	Marched to ANNEQUIN F.29 Sheet 36 B. arrived at 1 pm.	Jh.
ANNEQUIN			From this date the Battalion was attached to the 12th Division for working and carrying. Two companies were billeted in ANNEQUIN, one in VERMELLES, G.8. Sheet 36 c. and one company in LANCASHIRE TRENCH at G.2.b.5.0. Sheet 36 c. During the next three days the Battalion was employed clearing trenches and carrying bombs and R.E. material to the Battalions of the 12th Division in front of the HOHENZOLLERN REDOUBT (L.S. Sheet 36 b)	Jh.
	14.3.16	4.30 pm.	Left ANNEQUIN and marched to SAILLY-LABOURSE (L.3. Sheet 36 b) where 40 motor lorries were waiting which conveyed troops to BURBURE (C.3 Sheet 36 B) arriving 7.30 pm.	Jh.
BURBURE	17.3.16		A draft of 46 O.R. joined from 3rd Royal Sussex Regt.	Jh.
	26.3.16	8.30am.	Left BURBURE and marched to LILLERS where Battalion less Regt Transport entrained. Proceeded thence by train to NOEUX-LES-MINES K.18 Sheet 36 B. Arrived 11 am.	Jh.

Confidential

Army Form C. 2118
Sheet 2

WAR DIARY of 6th (S) Bn The Royal Irish Regt

INTELLIGENCE SUMMARY

(Erase heading not required.)

March 1916

Place	Date	Hour	Summary of Events and Information	Remarks and references to Appendices
NOEUX-LES-MINES	25.3.16		Regtl Transport travelled by road to NOEUX-LES-MINES.	JHL
LOOS (G.36. Sheet 36c.)		4.45 pm	Left NOEUX-LES-MINES and marched to LOOS and proceeded to take over the trenches then occupied by the 7th Royal Scots Fusiliers. Relief commenced at 7 pm from PHILOSOPHE and was complete at 10.20pm. The Battalion then held the right sub-section of the PUITS No 14 BIS Section from the junction of GORDON ALLEY with the front trench at H.31.C.3.0 Sheet 36c. to the junction of RAILWAY ALLEY and front trench at H.31.a.5.9. The line was held as follows :- Two companies in the front line - one Company in the support line about 70 yards behind the front line - and one company in the Reserve line about 500 yards behind the front line. Battalion Headquarters was in a cellar in LOOS. The Battalion was on the right of the 16th Division Front with the 7th Leinster Regt on our left. The 2nd Royal Munster Fusiliers was on our right being part of the 1st Division.	JHL
	25.3.16		Casualties - O.R. 1 killed, 3 wounded	JHL
	26.3.16		Casualties - O.R. 2 wounded	JHL

WAR DIARY of 6th (S) Bn. The Royal Irish Regt.

March 1916

Army Form C. 2118

Place	Date	Hour	Summary of Events and Information	Remarks and references to Appendices
LOOS	27.3.16		Casualties – Lt + Qm. J.C. WILLIAMS wounded also 1 O.R. wounded.	JH.
	28.3.16		Casualties – O.R. 2 wounded. The Battalion was relieved by the 6th Connaught Rangers. Relief commenced 8pm and was completed at 1.20am 29.3.16	JH. JH.
	29.3.16		After relief the Companies returned independently to PHILOSOPHE G.20.c Sheet 36c where the Battn reassembled in billets	JH.
PHILOSOPHE	30.3.16		Billets shelled. Casualties O.R. 1 wounded.	JH.
	31.3.16	2pm	47th Inf Brigade was relieved by 49th Inf Brigade and the battalion by the 8th Royal Inniskilling Fusiliers and handed to MAZANGARBE L.23. Sheet 36c/3. A draft of 30 O.R. joined from the 4th Royal Irish Regt.	JH. JH.

Sincerely Burgoyne
Lieut Colonel
Comdg 6th Royal Irish Regt.

Confidential — Original

WAR DIARY of 6th (S) Bn The Royal Irish Regiment
INTELLIGENCE SUMMARY
April 1916 — Vol 5

Army Form C. 2118.

Place	Date	Hour	Summary of Events and Information	Remarks and references to Appendices
MAZINGARBE	1.4.16		At the beginning of the month the Battalion was billeted in MAZINGARBE (L.23 Sheet 36B) and formed part of the Brigade in Reserve (i.e. 47th Inf Bde) behind that part of the line held by the 16th Division.	
	3.4.16	3pm	Billets were shelled. Casualties :— 1 OR killed, 7 OR wounded.	
	4.4.16		Capt A.E. WARMINGTON was sent to ENGLAND.	
	6.4.16		47th Brigade Relieved 48th Brigade in HULLOCH Sector from STONE STREET (G.12.d.7.2. Sheet 36c) to POSEN ALLEY (H.25.B.0.8.) 6th Royal Irish relieved the 9th Batt R. Dublin Fusiliers. Relief commenced at 5pm and was complete at 9pm. The Battalion was then distributed as follows :— Three companies and Battalion Headquarters were in TENTH AVENUE which runs along the LOOS - LA BASSÉE Road and were in Support to the 6th Connaught Rangers and 8th R Munster Fusiliers who were holding the front line. One company was in the Reserve Trench in front of TENTH AVENUE mentioned above a reserve to both the Battalions and constituted	
Trenches before HULLOCH	6.4.16		Casualties :— 1 OR killed, 3 OR wounded.	J.J.

Army Form C. 2118.
Sheet 2

WAR DIARY of 6th (S) Bn The Royal Irish Regiment
INTELLIGENCE SUMMARY.
April 1916

(Erase heading not required.)

Place	Date	Hour	Summary of Events and Information	Remarks and references to Appendices
Trenches before HULLOCH	8-4-16		Casualties :- Lieut J.E. DAY and 1 OR wounded.	
	9-4-16	1 pm	Relieved by 7th Bat Leinster Regt. Relief commenced 1 pm and was completed at 2 pm.	
			When relieved the Battalion in turn relieved the 6th Connaught Rangers in the right Sub Section. Relief commenced at 2 pm and was completed at 4.15 pm. The line then taken over was the front line trench from POSEN ALLEY (H.25.B.08, Sheet 36c) to HOLLY LANE (H.13.C.3.0). Three companies occupied the front trench and each of these companies found its own supports, which were kept in its Support trench. One company occupied the reserve trench. Battalion Head quarters was at G.24.C.O.9.	
	9.4.16		Casualties :- 1 OR wounded	
	10.4.16		Casualties :- 1 OR killed, 3 OR wounded	
	12.4.16		Casualties :- 1 OR wounded	
	13.4.16		Casualties :- 1 OR wounded	
	13.4.16		Casualties :- 1 OR wounded	

Confidential

WAR DIARY of 6th (S) Bn.
The Royal Irish Regiment

Army Form C. 2118.
Sheet 3.
April 1916

Instructions regarding War Diaries and Intelligence Summaries are contained in F. S. Regs., Part II. and the Staff Manual respectively. Title pages will be prepared in manuscript.

INTELLIGENCE SUMMARY.
(Erase heading not required.)

Place	Date	Hour	Summary of Events and Information	Remarks and references to Appendices
Trenches before HULLOCH	15-4-16	6.30 a.m.	Reserve Trench was heavily shelled. The officer commanding the Reserve Company Lieut T.V. BRODERICK was killed. Other casualties 6 OR killed, 5 OR wounded. During the afternoon the support of the line was heavily bombarded with rifle grenades and aerial torpedoes.	Ath.
	16-4-16	1 pm	The Battalion was relieved by the 6th Batt Connaught Rangers. Relief commenced at 1 p.m. and was complete at 3.40 p.m. On the completion of the relief the Battalion returned to PHILOSOPHE (G.13.d) and took over billets there	Ath.
	16-4-16		Casualties :- 3 OR wounded	Ath.
PHILOSOPHE	20-4-16	2 pm	Relieved by the 7th Battn R. Inniskilling Fusiliers and on completion of relief marched to NOEUX-LES-MINES (K.18. sheet 36B). This move formed part of the relief of the 47th Brigade by the 49th. The 47th Brigade on the completion of the relief became the Brigade in reserve of the 16th Division with 2 Battalions at NOEUX-LES-MINES and 2 battalions at MAZINGARBE	Ath.
NOEUX-LES-MINES	24-4-16		One man was accidentally wounded during Bombing Practice	Ath.

Confidential

Army Form C. 2118.

Instructions regarding War Diaries and Intelligence Summaries are contained in F.S. Regs., Part II. and the Staff Manual respectively. Title pages will be prepared in manuscript.

WAR DIARY
~~INTELLIGENCE~~ SUMMARY
(Erase heading not required.)

6th (S) Bn Sheet
The Royal Irish Regiment
April 1916

Place	Date	Hour	Summary of Events and Information	Remarks and references to Appendices
NOEUX LES MINES			Reference Sheet 36c.	
	27.4.16	5:10 a.m.	Under cover of gas and smoke the Germans attacked the line held by 16th Division from HOLLY LANE (H.13.c.3.1) to RAILWAY ALLEY (H.25.c.5.1). The alarm was given in NOEUX-LES-MINES and the 47th Inf. Brigade was held in readiness. The attack was repulsed without the aid of the 47th Inf. Brigade. Known at half an hour later.	W/o.
do	27.4.16	6.30 p.m.	The Germans again reached NOEUX-LES-MINES but did no damage. The enemy again launched gas over our lines and the alarm was given but no did not move.	W/o.
do	29.4.16	5:15 a.m.	The enemy again used gas but did not attack in this case. Some of the gas was blown back over his own trenches.	W/o.
do	29.4.16	7.30 p.m.	The 47th Inf. Brigade relieved the 48th Inf. Brigade in the PUITS 14 BIS sector. The Battalion relieved the 9th Royal Munster Fusiliers in the right subsection from RAILWAY ALLEY (H.25.c.5.1) to GORDON ALLEY (N.1.A.2.9). The line was held as follows:- Front line 3 Companies, finding their own supports, Reserve line 1 Coy. Battalion headquarters at LOOS at G.36.A.4.5. The relief commenced at 7.30	W/o.
LOOS	30.4.16		p.m. 29.4.16 from PHILOSOPHE and was complete at 12.30 a.m. 30.4.16. Casualties:- 2 O.R. killed 3 O.R. wounded.	W/o.

Lieut. Col
Comdg 6th Bn Royal Irish Regt

WAR DIARY
INTELLIGENCE SUMMARY

of 1st (S) Bn. The Royal Irish Regt.

May 1916

Place	Date	Hour	Summary of Events and Information	Remarks and references to Appendices
LOOS.			Reference Sheet 36 C	
	1.5.16		At the beginning of the month the Battn. was holding the front line from RAILWAY ALLEY (H.25.c.5.1) to GORDON ALLEY (N.1.A.2.9). Headquarters in LOOS Village. The 16th Division was on our right and the 8th MUNSTERS on our left.	Ap.
	1.5.16	8.38pm	Hot flew a small mine opposite GORDON ALLEY (N.1.A.29) about 40 yards from front line. A crater was formed about 10 feet high and 18 yards long. The crater was at once occupied by extra Vidt. Found depth C.B. MITCHELL wounded, 1 OR killed, 7 OR wounded.	Ap.
			Casualties :- 2 OR killed, 7 OR wounded.	Ap.
	2.5.16		Casualties :- Find depth C.B. MITCHELL wounded, 1 OR killed, 7 OR wounded.	Ap.
	3.5.16	8pm	Relieved by 6th CONNAUGHT RANGERS. Relief commenced at 8pm and was complete at 11.30pm. On completion of relief the battalion moved into Brigade support, and took up its position as follows:- 3 companies in 10th AVENUE from G.28.D to G.23.D.2.9, 1 company in GUN ALLEY from G.29.D.8.3 to G.24.D.3.0.	Ap.
SUPPORT TRENCHES			Casualties :- 4 OR killed, 5 OR wounded.	Ap.
	4.5.16		Casualties :- 1 OR killed.	Ap.
	7.5.16	8pm	Relieved 6th CONNAUGHT RANGERS in trenches which we had handed over to them on 3-5-16. Relief commenced 8pm and was complete at 10.30pm.	Ap.

B1059

SECRET

To
D.A.G.
3rd Echelon.
BASE

Herewith War Diary of my Battalion for May 1916

1.6.16

[signature]
Lieut Colonel
Comm'dg 6th Royal Irish Regt

6.J.

Original

Confidential

Army Form C. 2118.

Sheet 2

WAR DIARY of 6th (S) Bn. The Royal Irish Regt.

INTELLIGENCE SUMMARY

May 1916

(Erase heading not required.)

Instructions regarding War Diaries and Intelligence Summaries are contained in F.S. Regs., Part II. and the Staff Manual respectively. Title pages will be prepared in manuscript.

Place	Date	Hour	Summary of Events and Information	Remarks and references to Appendices
LOOS			Reference Sheet 36 c	
	8.5.16		Casualties — 1 OR killed and 1 OR wounded.	"
	9.5.16	1.30 am	The enemy carried out a small raid on our trenches. A party of about 15 Germans entered our trenches at the head of SCOTS ALLEY at H.31.c.7.6. They were quickly driven out but all escaped. Casualties — 4 OR killed, 6 OR wounded	"
	10.5.16		Casualties — 2 OR killed, 6 OR wounded	" "
	11.5.16	11.30 am	Our front trench was heavily bombarded by the enemy for half an hour with large shells. Much damage was done to LOOS was bombarded on our left very heavily attacked. The village with lachrymatory shells Casualties — 4 OR killed 7 OR wounded.	" " "
	12.5.16	9 pm	Bn was relieved by 6th CONNAUGHT RANGERS. Relief commenced at 9 pm and was complete at 11 pm. On completion of relief, the Battalion moved into Brigade Support and again occupied the trenches which we left on 7.5.16. Casualties — 1 OR wounded.	" " "

Original

Army Form C. 2118.

WAR DIARY of 6TH (S) B.
~~INTELLIGENCE SUMMARY~~
The Royal Irish Regiment
May 1916
Sheet 3.

(Erase heading not required.)

Confidential
Instructions regarding War Diaries and Intelligence Summaries are contained in F.S. Regs., Part II. and the Staff Manual respectively. Title pages will be prepared in manuscript.

Place	Date	Hour	Summary of Events and Information	Remarks and references to Appendices
			Reference Sheet 36.c.	
SUPPORT TRENCHES	16.5.16	1.30pm	Relieved by 9th Royal Munster Fusiliers. On relief Battalion Headquarters and two Companies moved into billets in MAZINGARBE (L.23). Two Companies moved into Billets in PHILOSOPHE (G.20) — Sheet 36.B.	JM
MAZINGARBE	17.5.16		The two Companies which were in PHILOSOPHE moved to MAZINGARBE. During 16th and 17th the 47th Infantry Brigade was relieved by the 48th Infantry Brigade and became Reserve Brigade.	JM
	25.5.16		Relieved 9th Royal Munster Fusiliers in right Sub-Section 14 Bis Section. This move formed part of the relief of 48th Inf Brigade by 47th Inf Brigade. We then occupied the front line from ENGLISH ALLEY (H.31.A.5.2) to the CHALK PIT at H.25.B.2.3.	JM
TRENCHES N.E. OF LOOS			The front line was held by 3 Companies, with one in Support. Battalion Headquarters was in GUN ALLEY at G.36.B.2.8. The 49th Brigade was on our right and the 8th MUNSTERS on our left.	JM
	26.5.16		Casualties – 2 OR wounded.	
	27.5.16		A deserter was captured by the 1st Division on our right. He stated	JM

Confidential
Original
Army Form C. 2118.

WAR DIARY
of 6th (S) Bn.
The Royal Irish Regt.
Sheet 4.

INTELLIGENCE SUMMARY

May 1916

(Erase heading not required.)

Instructions regarding War Diaries and Intelligence Summaries are contained in F.S. Regs., Part II. and the Staff Manual respectively. Title pages will be prepared in manuscript.

Place	Date	Hour	Summary of Events and Information	Remarks and references to Appendices
TRENCHES N.E. of LOOS	27.5.16		Reference Sheet 36 c. That the enemy was preparing to attack our line. The Battalion was consequently reinforced by 1 company from the 6th Connaught Rangers. Casualties — 1 O.R. wounded.	9/h
	28.5.16	7 p.m	Our front and support trenches were subjected to a severe bombardment with shells, grenades and heavy trench mortars. The total damage was done to our trenches from 7 p.m. to 7.45 p.m. Casualties — 2 O.R. killed, 12 O.R. wounded.	9/h
	29.5.16		The Battalion was relieved by the 6th Connaught Rangers. Relief commenced at 4.30 p.m. but owing to the bad state of the trenches it was not complete until 10.30 p.m. Two companies however remained in the RESERVE TRENCH to support the 7th Leinster Regt in view of the expected attack. The remainder of the Battalion retiring into Brigade Support into 10th AVENUE and one in GUN ALLEY. Two companies of the 8th Royal Munster Fusiliers were	9/h

Original

Confidential

Army Form C. 2118.

WAR DIARY of 5 / 6th CB Bn.
The Royal Irish Regt.
INTELLIGENCE SUMMARY.
(Erase heading not required.)

May 1916
Sheet 5.

Instructions regarding War Diaries and Intelligence Summaries are contained in F.S. Regs, Part II. and the Staff Manual respectively. Title pages will be prepared in manuscript.

Place	Date	Hour	Summary of Events and Information	Remarks and references to Appendices
TRENCHES N.Q.Loos	29.5.16		Attached kg to replace those detached. Casualties - 1 OR killed 6 OR wounded	ffh.
	30.5.16		Casualties - 6 OR wounded	ffh.
	31.5.16		Two platoons were withdrawn from the company supporting 1st 9th Leinster Regt and joined the Battalion in 10th AVENUE.	ffh.

Sidney Burgoyne
Lieut Colonel
Commdg 6th Royal Irish Regt.

SECRET

To
Officer in Charge
Adjutant General's Office
Base

2 JUL 1916
1972

Herewith War Diary (Original) of my Battalion for the month of June 1916.

B.E.F.
1/7/16

[signature] Lieut Colonel
Commg 6th Royal West [Regt]

SECRET

Instructions regarding War Diaries and Intelligence Summaries are contained in F.S. Regs., Part II. and the Staff Manual respectively. Title pages will be prepared in manuscript.

WAR DIARY of 6th (S) Bn. The Royal Irish Regiment

INTELLIGENCE SUMMARY.
(Erase heading not required.)

Army Form C. 2118.
June 1916
Vol 7

Place	Date	Hour	Summary of Events and Information	Remarks and references to Appendices
Trenches near PUITS 14 BIS	1/6/16		Reference Sheet 36c. At the commencement of the month the 47th Inf Brigade was holding the part of the line known as the "PUITS 14 BIS" Section which ran from H.19.A.3.3. to H.31.A.6.2. Two battalions held the front line with one in support and one in reserve. The reserve battalion only consisted however of 2 companies as the battalions in the front line had been each reinforced by 1 company in view of an attack which was thought possible. The 6th Royal Irish Regt were — Support in trenches running along the high ground from Sq. G.28.d. to Sq. G.23.d. Two companies had been sent to reinforce the battalions in the front line and these had been replaced by 2 companies from the Reserve Battalion. The front line was held by the 6th Connaught Rangers on the right and the 7th Leinster on the left. The 8th Munsters were in Reserve at PHILOSOPHE (G.20.a.) Casualties :— 1 OR wounded	✓
	2/6/16	2 pm	Relieved 6th Connaught in Right Sub-section of the front line. Relief commenced at 2 pm and was complete at 10.30 pm. The line then held ran from now as PUITS 14 BIS from H.25.B.1.4. to H.31.A.6.2. and	✓

Original

Army Form C. 2118.
Sheet 2

WAR DIARY

of 6th (S) Bn
The Royal Irish Regiment
June 1916

~~INTELLIGENCE~~ SUMMARY.
(Erase heading not required.)

SECRET

Instructions regarding War Diaries and Intelligence Summaries are contained in F. S. Regs., Part II. and the Staff Manual respectively. Title pages will be prepared in manuscript.

Place.	Date	Hour	Summary of Events and Information	Remarks and references to Appendices
Trenches near Potts 14.B18	2/6/16		And was held as follows. Three companies held the front line, find-ing their own supports and one company was kept in the Reserve Line. In addition to the latter a company of the 8th Hampshires was placed at our disposal and was also kept in reserve.	#ta
			Casualties :- 3 OR killed and 2 wounded	#ta
	3/6/16	11 AM	The Ammunition trench known as POPE'N ALLEY and the ground near Battalion Headquarters was heavily shelled for 2 hours with 8" shells. About 60 shells were fired of which half, so failed to explode	#ta
			Casualties :- 2 OR killed and 6 OR wounded	#ta
	4/6/16	1 AM	Our field-guns carried out a bombardment of the enemy from trenches lasting half an hour. There was very little retaliation.	#ta
			Casualties :- 3 OR killed and 1 OR wounded	#ta
	5/6/16		Casualties :- 1 OR killed and 4 OR wounded	#ta
	6/6/16	11 AM	The enemy commenced a severe bombardment of our supports and communication trenches lasting until 12.30 pm. A dug-out was blown in burying several men. These were all dug out except four who could not be recovered	#ta

Original

Army Form C. 2118.
Sheet 3

SECRET

WAR DIARY
or
INTELLIGENCE SUMMARY.

of 6th (S) Bn. The Royal Irish Regiment

June 1916.

(Erase heading not required.)

Instructions regarding War Diaries and Intelligence Summaries are contained in F.S. Regs., Part II. and the Staff Manual respectively. Title pages will be prepared in manuscript.

Place	Date	Hour	Summary of Events and Information	Remarks and references to Appendices
Trenches near PUITS 14 BIS	6/6/16		Casualties :- 5 OR killed, 11 OR wounded.	ill.
		8.30pm	Relieved by 6th Connaught. Relief commenced 8.30 pm and completed at 11.25 pm. To which E Battalion and became Battalion in Reserve to Support Battalion. Two companies however remained in trenches attached to the Support Battalion	ill.
PHILOSOPHE	7/6/16		Casualties :- 1 OR killed, 2 OR wounded. These Casualties occurred in the Companies attached to the Support Battalion.	ill.
	8/6/16		Bn of the Companies attached to the Support Battalion was withdrawn to PHILOSOPHE.	ill. ill.
	9/6/16		Casualties :- 1 OR killed	
	10/6/16		The 47th Inf Brigade was relieved by the 49th Inf Brigade and moved into reserve. The 6th Royal Irish were relieved by the 8th Royal Fusiliers at 3.30 pm and marched to NOEUX-LES-MINES (Sheet 36 B K.18.D) arriving at 4.45 pm	ill. ill.
	10/6/16		Casualties :- 2 OR killed, 1 OR wounded	ill.
NOEUX-LES-MINES	11/6/16		During the next 7 days training in musketry, bombing, bayonet fighting etc was carried on	ill.

Original

Army Form C. 2118.
Sheet 4.

WAR DIARY
or
INTELLIGENCE SUMMARY

SECRET

Instructions regarding War Diaries and Intelligence Summaries are contained in F.S. Regs., Part II. and the Staff Manual respectively. Title pages will be prepared in manuscript.

of 6 R(B) Res.
The Royal Irish Regt
June 1916

(Erase heading not required.)

Place	Date	Hour	Summary of Events and Information	Remarks and references to Appendices
NOEUX-LES-MINES	16/6/16		The 47th Inf. Brigade relieved the 48th Inf. Brigade in the LOOS Section of the front line extending from M.S.D.3.9. to H.31.A.6.3. (Sheet 36C) The 6th Royal Irish Regt relieved the 1st Royal Munster Fusiliers in the left Subsection extending from H.31.A.6.3. to M.6.B.3.6. (Sheet 36.C.)	
LOOS	17/6/16		The line was held with 3 companies in the front line finding their own supports and one company in reserve. Battalion headquarters were in LOOS (G.36.A.). The relief commenced from PHILOSOPHE at 6pm and was complete at 11.35pm. No Sergeant T. CAHILL was awarded the D.C.M. and No Private J. BRYANT the Military Medal.	
	18/6/16		Casualties :- 3 O.R. killed, 5 O.R. wounded. There occurred a bombardment of our front trenches with heavy Trench Mortars in front of our line. There were six small craters now in front occupied by us. The enemy was working on them every night in order to consolidate them. A raid was arranged on the most northern of these called CAMERON CRATER (H.31.C.4.1.). A party consisting of	
	19/6/16	11.30pm		

Original

SECRET

Army Form C. 2118.

WAR DIARY of 6th (S) Bn.
The Royal Irish Regt.
INTELLIGENCE SUMMARY. June 1916

Sheet 5

Instructions regarding War Diaries and Intelligence
Summaries are contained in F.S. Regs., Part II.
and the Staff Manual respectively. Title pages
will be prepared in manuscript.

(Erase heading not required.)

Place	Date	Hour	Summary of Events and Information	Remarks and references to Appendices
LOOS	19/6/16		2nd Lieut CLARIDGE, 2nd Lt. GOWTHORPE and 15 OR. carried out the raid in a most successful manner. They succeeded in killing the Sentries on to date and in surprising and bombing a large enemy working party. Who suffered heavy casualties. He had no killed but lost officers and several men were wounded, all of whom were got back to our own trenches. Congratulations were received from both Brigadier and the Divisional General on the success of the enterprise. Casualties :- Lieut D.R. CLARIDGE, 2nd Lt R.W. GOWTHORPE and 10 OR. wounded	JHM
	19/6/16			JHM
	20/6/16		A quiet day. Casualties :- 1 OR. wounded killed	JHM
	21/6/16	9.30 p	Relieved by 6th Connaught Rangers. Relief was complete at 12.20 a 22/6/16. On the completion of the relief the Battalion moved to PHILOSOPHE and became battalion in reserve	JHM
	21/6/16		Casualties :- 1 OR. wounded	JHM
PHILOSOPHE	24/6/16	7 pm	Left PHILOSOPHE and moved up to LOOS to relieve the 6th Connaught Rangers in the trenches which we had vacated on June 21st. Relief	JHM

Original
Army Form C. 2118.
Sheet 5
June 1916

WAR DIARY of 6th (S) Bn
The Royal Irish Regiment

INTELLIGENCE SUMMARY
(Erase heading not required.)

Instructions regarding War Diaries and Intelligence Summaries are contained in F.S. Regs., Part II. and the Staff Manual respectively. Title pages will be prepared in manuscript.

Place	Date	Hour	Summary of Events and Information	Remarks and references to Appendices
LOOS	24/6/16		Ref Sheet 36c. Relief complete at 12.30 a.m.	
	25/6/16		The line was held in the same way as during the previous turn, the 7th Leinster Regt being on our right and the 49th Inf Brigade on our left. During the day preparations were made for a combined Gas and Smoke attack to take place the following morning if the wind was very favourable. Gas cylinders had previously been put in position along the front line trenches by the Royal Engineers from our left to SCOTS REDT (H.31.C.6.7) to our left, they extended over the whole front occupied by the 16th Division. The arrangements were as follows :-	
		1 a.m.	Discharge of gas	
		1.10 a.m.	Commence Smoke Cloud with Smoke Candles	
		1.15 a.m.	Turn off gas	
		1.15 to 1.25 a.m.	Continue Smoke cloud with Smoke Candles	
		1.45 a.m.	Send out a patrol to examine the enemy wire and ascertain the novelle produced	
		At 11.30 p.m.	Howard was so feeble and uncertain that it was	

Original

Army Form C. 2118.
Sheet 7

WAR DIARY
INTELLIGENCE SUMMARY.
of 6th (S) Bn.
The Royal Irish Regiment
June 1916

(Erase heading not required.)

Instructions regarding War Diaries and Intelligence Summaries are contained in F. S. Regs., Part II. and the Staff Manual respectively. Title pages will be prepared in manuscript.

SECRET

Place	Date	Hour	Summary of Events and Information	Remarks and references to Appendices
Loos	23/6/16		Rf Sheet 36c decided to postpone the attack. Casualties:- 2 OR wounded.	Apps
	25/6/16		Preparations were again made to carry out the gas attack but it had again to be postponed on account of the wind.	Apps
	26/6/16		Casualties:- 2 OR killed, 5 OR wounded.	Apps
	27/6/16	12.15AM	Following on the explosion by 2 mines by the 7th Leinsters on our right caused by a successful raid on the enemy trenches between one prison and killing some hundreds of the enemy. During the raid the two craters were consolidated and the raiding party returned at dawn. This provoked some retaliation from the enemy on our along our front causing some casualties.	Apps
	27/6/16		Casualties:- Lieut J.H. FALLA and 2nd Lieut O. CROSBIE wounded also 2 OR killed and 13 OR wounded	Apps
	28/6/16	1am	It was decided to carry out the gas attack at 1 am at the last moment however the officer responsible for liberating the gas decided that the wind was not suitable and no gas was liberated	

Original
Army Form C. 2118.
Sheet 8

WAR DIARY
of 6th (S) Bn.
The Royal Irish Regiment
INTELLIGENCE SUMMARY.
June 1916

(Erase heading not required.)

Place	Date	Hour	Summary of Events and Information	Remarks and references to Appendices
LOOS	28/6/16		Ref Sheet 36 c. On the battalion front. It was however directed on our left and the Sunder programme was carried out but no patrol was sent out. The Artillery retaliation was slight.	
	29/6/16		Casualties :- 9 O.R. wounded	
	29/6/16	6.30p	We trained to enemy's front line opposite Scott Alley with Rifle Grenades and Trench Mortar bombs. They were slight retaliation from enemies Artillery and trench mortar.	
		8.30p	Relieved by 8th Connaught Rangers. Relief complete at 11.25 p.m. on completion of relief Battalion moved into PHILOSOPHE. Casualties :- 10R killed, 7OR. wounded.	
PHILOSOPHE	30/6/16	9.15p	The 3rd Inf Brigade on our right carried out a small attack. Some prisoners were taken but no ground was gained. An enemy exploded two big mines under their front trench. The 16th Divisional Artillery assisted.	

Sidney Long
Lieut Colonel
Comdg 6th Royal Irish Regt.

W A R   D I A R Y

6th (S) Bn The
Royal Irish Rgt.

1st. July to 31st. July 1916.

VOLUME No. 8

Original

SECRET   Army Form C. 2118.

Instructions regarding War Diaries and Intelligence
Summaries are contained in F.S. Regs., Part II.
and the Staff Manual respectively. Title pages
will be prepared in manuscript.

WAR DIARY
or
INTELLIGENCE SUMMARY.
(Erase heading not required.)

Army Form C. 2118.
Sheet 1

81st Bde.   The Royal Irish Regiment   July 1916

Place	Date	Hour	Summary of Events and Information	Remarks and references to Appendices
PHILOSOPHE	1/7/16		At the beginning of the month the Battalion was billeted in PHILOSOPHE (G.20.a, Sheet 36c). The 47th Inf Brigade was holding the Front Line from ENGLISH Avenue (H.19.a.6.2 Sheet 36c) to HAYMARKET (M.5.d.4.9, Sheet 36c) known at the Loos Sector. The 8th Royal Irish was Reserve Battalion.	A/4
	2/7/16		A quiet day. Casualties :- 1 O.R. wounded	A/4
	3/7/16	3pm	The 47th Inf Brigade was relieved by the 49th Inf Brigade and moved into Divisional Reserve. The 8th Royal Irish was relieved by the 8th Royal Inniskilling Fusiliers and moved to MAZINGARBE where they occupied huts. (L.23.9 Sheet 36c)	A/4
MAZINGARBE	3/7/16	5pm	The huts which we had just occupied were shelled and some damage was done. Casualties :- 1 O.R. wounded	A/4
	4/7/16	11am	Huts again shelled. Casualties :- 2 O.R. wounded.	A/4
	5/7/16	11am	Huts Shelled — no casualties.	A/4
	7/7/16	10.3pm	Town of MAZINGARBE was shelled heavily for about 15 minutes.	A/4
	8/7/16		An accident occurred during practice in firing Rifle Grenades, 2 Pte's became casualties, Capt A.D. PLACE at a C.P. Exploding prematurely and wounding Capt A.D. PLACE in both thighs in Arm 7A 1315 shooting.	A/4
	11/7/16		The 47th Inf Brigade relieved the 48th Inf Brigade in front of	

Original

Army Form C. 2118.
Sheet 2

WAR DIARY
of 6TH (S) Bn
The Royal Irish Regiment
July 1916

INTELLIGENCE SUMMARY.
(Erase heading not required.)

Place	Date	Hour	Summary of Events and Information	Remarks and references to Appendices
MAZINGARBE	11/7/16		Ref. Sheet 36c of the front line from KENDAL ALLEY (H.19.a.8.3) to ENGLISH ALLEY (H.31.a.6.2). The 6th Royal Irish moved into the right sub-section when it relieved the 7th Royal Irish Rifles. Relief commenced at 6pm and was complete at 6.30 pm. The line then occupied extended from H.25b.23 to ENGLISH ALLEY. Three companies held the front line and one occupied the Reserve trench. Battalion Headquarters was situated in the Reserve line.	A/s
Trenches from PUITS 14 BIS	12/7/16		The 49th Inf. Brigade was on our right and the 7th Leinster on our left. There was an intermittent bombardment during the day with shells, trench mortars and rifle grenades. Casualties – 2 OR killed, 13 OR wounded	A/s
	13/7/16		Trenches were again shelled at intervals. Casualties – 2 OR killed 3 OR wounded	A/s
	14/7/16		The day passed more quietly but there was some bombardment. Casualties – 1 OR killed, 3 OR wounded	A/s
			The constant bombardment assisted by bad weather has greatly damaged our trenches in spite of the constant work being done on them by our men	A/s

SECRET

WAR DIARY OF 6**(S) Bn The Royal Irish Regiment**

INTELLIGENCE SUMMARY July 1916 Sheet-3

Army Form C. 2118

Place	Date	Hour	Summary of Events and Information	Remarks and references to Appendices
Trenches near Ports 14 B15	15/7/16	2.30pm	Ref. Street 36c. Relieved by 6th Connaught Rangers. Relief commenced at 2.30pm and was complete at 5.30pm. On completion of Relief the Battalion moved into Brigade Support and occupied trenches known as 10TH AVENUE running along the high ground from H.23.b to H.28.b.	
	15/7/16		Casualties:— 6 OR wounded. A draft of 84 NCOs and men joined from the base. The 4 days during which the Battalion was in Brigade Support passed quietly and there were no casualties. The men were employed chiefly in working on and carrying stores and ammunition to the front trenches.	
	19/7/16	2pm	Relieved 6th Connaught Rangers in Right Sub-Section. Relief commenced at 2pm and was complete at 5pm. The Bn was held in the same way as during the previous tour. The 48th Brigade were on our Right and the 8th Royal Munster Fusiliers on our Left. During the night of the 19TH/20TH the 6th Royal Munster Fusiliers on our Left carried out a successful raid and succeeded in cutting up enemy trenches, doing considerable damage	

SECRET

Army Form C. 2118

Instructions regarding War Diaries and Intelligence Summaries are contained in F.S. Regs., Part II and the Staff Manual respectively. Title Pages will be prepared in manuscript.

WAR DIARY or INTELLIGENCE SUMMARY
(Erase heading not required.)

6th (S) Bn. The Royal Irish Regiment

July 1916   Sheet 4.

Place	Date	Hour	Summary of Events and Information	Remarks and references to Appendices
Trenches near PUITS 14 BIS	20/7/16		Ref Sheet 36 C. Quiet day. Casualties :- 2 OR wounded	4/4.
	21/7/16	5.15pm	Our line was heavily shelled with 4.2 in. Shells. This continued until 6pm. Casualties :- 2 OR killed and 4 OR wounded.	4/4.
	22/7/16		The 48th Inf Brigade on Bn right was relieved by the 121st Brigade belonging to the 40th Division.	4/4.
		11.30pm	We carried out a small raid on the enemy's sap known as Y 3 at H.31.6.1.6. Two parties each consisting of 1 Officer and 12 OR and each carrying a Bangalore torpedo left our trench to attempt to blow up the enemy's wire and enter his trench. In this they were not successful. Both torpedoes were successfully exploded in the enemy's wire but the wire was not completely cut and the party were unable to enter the trench. Bombs were thrown in to the trench as to paralyse any hostile reply and at 1.5 am 23rd having only suffered one casualty, -- an officer being slightly wounded, returned to our trench. Casualties :- 2nd Lieut T.E. MAGILL and 3 OR wounded.	4/4.
	23/7/16		A Quiet day. Casualties :- 1 OR killed, 3 OR wounded	4/4.

Army Form C. 2118

WAR DIARY
or
INTELLIGENCE SUMMARY

(Erase heading not required.)

of 5th (S) Bn.
The Royal Irish Regiment
July 1916
Sheet 5

Place	Date	Hour	Summary of Events and Information	Remarks and references to Appendices
Trenches near PUITS 14 BIS.	29/7/16		Ref. Sheets 36b + C. There was some activity on both sides with Trench Mortars during the day. Casualties:- 1 OR wounded	
	30/7/16		Relieved by 6th Connaught Rangers. Relief commenced at 2.20 p.m. and was complete at 4.30 p.m. On relief the Battalion moved again into Brigade Support in 10th AVENUE. Casualties:- 2 OR killed and 4 OR wounded	
			From 25th to 31st the Battalion remained in Brigade Support and was employed in working and carrying to the Battalions in the front line. No shelling was experienced and there were no casualties.	
	31/7/16	12 noon	The 47th Inf Bde was relieved by the 49th Inf Bde and moved into Divisional Reserve. The 5th Royal Irish Regt. was relieved by the 7th Royal Irish Fusiliers and marched to NOEUX-LES-MINES (2.13. Sheet 36 B)	
NOEUX-LES-MINES		5.30 p.m.	Arriving at 5.30 p.m. and took up billets in the town. Casualties: 1 OR killed and 1 OR wounded (both attached to other units)	

Lindsay Cougen Lieut-Colonel
Comm. dg. 5th Royal Irish Regt.

Vol 9

WAR DIARY.

6th Royal Irish Regiment.

MONTH OF AUGUST, 1916.

VOLUME:— "9"

WAR DIARY of 6th (S) Batt. Royal Irish Regiment

Army Form C. 2118

INTELLIGENCE SUMMARY

August 1916   Sheet 1.

Place	Date	Hour	Summary of Events and Information	Remarks and references to Appendices
NOEUX-LES-MINES	1/8/16		At the beginning of the month the 47th Inf Brigade was in Divisional Reserve. The 6th Royal Irish Regt was billeted in NOEUX-LES-MINES (K.18 Sheet 36.c.13) and was accommodated partly in huts and partly in the town. Whilst the Battn lived in NOEUX-LES-MINES training in bombing, wiring, musketry and other branches was continued.	Nil
	9/8/16		The 16th DIVISION took over more of the front line from the 40th DIVISION and the 47th Inf Brigade moved up to relieve the 120th Inf Brigade in the front line from CAMEROON ALLEY (H.31.c.6.1) to HAYMARKET (M.5.D.4.9) Sheet 36.c, N.E. of LOOS.	Nil
	9/8/16	5:30 p.m.	The 6th Royal Irish Regt took over the line between PICADILLY (M.6.B.1.5) and HAYMARKET from the 14th Argyll and Sutherland Highlanders and 14th Highland Light Infantry. This relief was complete at 11:30 p.m.	Nil
LOOS			The line held included two large craters known as HARTS (M.6.C.8.9) and HARRISONS (M.6.C.2.6) and the trenches were in a very damaged condition. Three companies held the front line and one kept in Reserve. Battalion headquarters were at (G.35.A.5.5)	Nil

WAR DIARY or INTELLIGENCE SUMMARY

of 6th (S) Battn. Royal Irish Regt.

August 1916   Sheet 2

Army Form C. 2118

Place	Date	Hour	Summary of Events and Information	Remarks and references to Appendices
LOOS	9/8/16		The 7th Leinsters were on our left and part of the 120th Inf Brigade on our right.	nil
	10/8/16		During the day the enemy displayed considerable activity with heavy trench-mortars and aerial torpedoes. We replied vigorously with trench mortars and artillery. Casualties:- 2 O.R. killed, 3 O.R. wounded.	nil
	11/8/16		The enemy was again active with trench mortars. Casualties:- 5 O.R. killed, 11 O.R. wounded.	nil
	12/8/16		The day passed more quietly. Casualties :- Capt. C.J. DAVIS wounded. 1 O.R. killed, 1 O.R. wounded.	nil
	13/8/16		The 6th Royal Irish Regt was relieved by the 6th Connaught Rangers. The relief commenced at 2.30 p.m. and was completed at 10 p.m. When relieved the Battalion moved into Brigade Reserve at MAZINGARBE.	nil
	17/8/16		The 6th Royal Irish Regt moved into the right sub-section and relieved the 8th Connaught Rangers. Whilst taking over trenches, LT. J.G. McILWRAITH and 2/LT. L.R. McCARTHY-BARRY were wounded, 4 O.R. killed, 4 O.R. wounded, all by an aerial torpedo.	1B.
	19/8/16		The enemy as usual was active with aerial torpedoes & heavy trench mortars, but did little damage. In the evening LT. A.V. BRIDGE & 2/LT. P.K. DOYLE were wounded whilst on reconnaissance.	1B.

SECRET

Army Form C. 2118

WAR DIARY
or
INTELLIGENCE SUMMARY
(Erase heading not required.)

Place	Date	Hour	Summary of Events and Information	Remarks and references to Appendices
LOOS.	21.8.16 22.8.16		The 6th Royal Irish Regt. carried out a raid to the East of HARRISONS CRATER, with the assistance of a mine. The mine was blown at 2 a.m. & the raiding party, under 2/Lt KELLY were on the enemy's trenches within the minute. Bangalore torpedoes were arranged for but owing to the tone of all the officers commanding the parties the leap for of all kinds fire parties did more arduous work objective. He is a man really party were unknown after hunting down several dug-outs in which objectionably 2/Lt R.S.KELLY S/O.R several casualties amongst the enemy, unfortunately 2/Lt R.S.KELLY S/O.R in safe guarding the withdrawal of this party was reported missing. Believed to be prisoner on a German road morning. Wounded on dying ("Tommy") we have one officer and 2/Lt man MC.) Lt.BN. FITZGIBBON was killed whilst in charge of M.G. & Lt.BYRNE was also killed when i/c of one of the Bangalore parties. S.O.R. killed 4/Lt M.A.HURLEY wounded and 18 O.R. 2/2 TOKFEEGAN and A.O.C PATMAN not—Back, 20.O.R. missing	13
			At 9.15 p.m. the B? was relieved by the 6th CONNAUGHT RANGERS and went into Brigade support (PREVITE PASSAGE) The day has passed quietly. Casualties 4 O.R. wounded	13
	22.8.16		Orders arrived for the Bn Division to be relieved by the 40th Division The 6th Royal Irish to be relieved by the 18th Welsh Regt The Last two days have been very quiet here.	13
MOEUX-LES-MINES	24.8.16		At 11.15 a.m. The Battalion was relieved by the 18th Welsh Regt The Battalion was billeted for the night at NOEUX-LES-MINES Total casualties of the Battalion since landing in France to date are:- 107 killed 352 wounded 5 missing TOTAL = 464.	13

SECRET

Army Form C. 2118

WAR DIARY or INTELLIGENCE SUMMARY

of 6 (S) Bⁿ Royal Irish Rgt.   Sheet 4

(Erase heading not required.)

Place	Date	Hour	Summary of Events and Information	Remarks and references to Appendices
MARLES-LES-MINES	25.8.16		At 11.30 the Bⁿ marched to MARLES-LES-MINES, arriving there at 2.30 p.m. same date, and were billeted for the night.	B.
BURBURE	26.8.16		At 11.30 a.m. the Bⁿ paraded for march to BURBURE, arrived there at 1.15 p.m. & were billeted for the night.	B.
" "	28.8.16		The 27th passed very quietly. On the 28th the Battalion occurred orders to march to CHOCQUES and entrain there for HEILLY. The Battalion left BURBURE at 12 midnight.	B.
SAND-PIT nr MEAULTE	29.8.16		At 2 a.m. The Battalion entrained at CHOCQUES arriving at HEILLY on the same day at 9.30 p.m. At 4.30 p.m. the Battalion paraded & marched to SAND-PIT, 1 mile S.E. of MEAULTE. During this march the weather both the Battalion experienced a violent thunderstorm and torrential rain. The Battalion bivouacked at SAND-PIT for the night.	B.
CARNOY	30.8.16		At 11 a.m. the Battalion moved to CITADEL CAMP, 2 miles from BRAY SUR-SOMME, where they halted for dinner, then at 5.20 p.m. the Bⁿ bivouacked 600 north of east of CARNOY in reserve to the 47th B^{de}.	B.

SECRET

WAR DIARY of 6th (S) Bn Royal Irish Regt.

Army Form C. 2118

Instructions regarding War Diaries and Intelligence Summaries are contained in F. S. Regs., Part II. and Staff Manual respectively. Title Pages will be prepared in manuscript.

INTELLIGENCE SUMMARY

(Erase heading not required.)

Place	Date	Hour	Summary of Events and Information	Remarks and references to Appendices
CARNOY	31-8-16		The day passed quietly for the Bn. This ends the DIARY for the month of August 1916.	
			V. E. Ward Simpson Capt comdg 6th (S) Bn The Royal Irish Regt.	

SAND PIT
MEAULTE

CARNOY

WAR DIARY.

6th Royal Irish Regiment

MONTH OF SEPTEMBER, 1916.

VOLUME :- 10

SECRET

WAR DIARY
or
INTELLIGENCE SUMMARY

Army Form C. 2118

of 6(S) Bn Royal Irish Regt.
September 1916. Sheet No. 1/2.

Place	Date	Hour	Summary of Events and Information	Remarks and references to Appendices
CARNOY	1-9-16		The Battalion moved from CARNOY to TRONES & SHERWOOD TRENCH.	
"	2-9-16		Received orders from the 47th INF. BDE for the attack on GUILLEMONT.	
"	3-9-16	At 12.3.p.m.	The Bⁿ advanced to the attack on GUILLEMONT via SUNKEN ROAD, which later was their final objective. The Bⁿ went over the parapet with their pipes playing & the men advanced in excellent order. The final objective was in our hands by 3 and 3-p.m. and the line was consolidated & held in spite of three counter attacks.	
GUILLEMONT			The casualties in the days fighting were heavy, being 14 officers & 311 O.R. 2/LT MAGILL & 2/LT DOWNING killed in action. MAJOR U.S. NAYLOR, 2/LT MOORE, 2/LT LLOYD, 2/LT MOORE died of wounds later.	
CARNOY	4-9-16	About 2.30 a.m.	The Bⁿ was relieved by the 12th K.R.R.C. & marched into bivouacs at CARNOY. CAPT & 2/LT K.R.R.C. MOORE died of wounds in 21st C.C.S. CAPT & 2/LT V.C. MOORE	
SUNKEN ROAD	7-9-16		The Bⁿ went into the line & took over trenches occupied by 5 & INNISKILLINGS FUSILIERS.	
"	8-9-16		Active artillery fire on both sides for most of the day. Received orders for the attack on following day.	

SECRET

WAR DIARY of 6th (S) Bn, Royal Irish Regt.

INTELLIGENCE SUMMARY

Army Form C. 2118

September 1916   Sheet 2.

Place	Date	Hour	Summary of Events and Information	Remarks and references to Appendices
SUNKEN ROAD	9/9/16		The 6th Royal Irish Regt with the rest of the 47th Bde made their rendezvous within a wood. Objective GINCHY. 47th Infy Bde advancing on the right front INF. BDE. on the left at 4.45 p.m. the attack commenced, 6 Royal Irish, 18 K.R. Munster Fusiliers on their left leading. The enemy however was found well prepared and the German enemy entrenched Germans on Northern banks of the counter attack of their machine guns doing the damage. From Ginchy this counter attack and on spot of further attempts the Bn head could not be captured. At 7.15 p.m. the 7 Innskilling Fuss were ordered to reinforce, and members had this had already been done and a further advance was thought not to be impracticable. The 5 can of General Rutradion up till dawn had many the 6th Bn was relieved by the 4th Grenadier Guards. The casualties suffered by the 6th Bn were Major, Lt Col F. Curzon, 2/Lt F.S.R. HACKETT, 2/LT J. HENNESSY, LT.E.A. STOKER and CAPT. & ADJT H. MALCOMSON (since died of wounds) & 38 OR killed; 6 officers & 104 OR wounded, LT P.F. CROSS & 2/LT F.A. HARRISON and 38 OR missing. Total 13 officers & 164 OR. Total casualties during period at the SOMME = 28 officers & 451 O.R.	S.
	10/9/16		On relief the OC marched back to CARNOY AREA. Lt Col & 2 i/c the Bn being wounded, the command of the Bn devolved to Major Macleod who had now arrived to HAPPY VALLEY & proceeded there for the night. 2/Lt NORTH join from the 3rd Bn joined the Bn.	S.
CARNOY	10/9/16		Bn at 3.45 p.m. the 6 Royal Irish with the rest of the 15th Bde marched to VAUX SUR-SOMME and billetted there. LT. E.A STOKER died of wounds at 21st C.C.S. on 12 Sept 1916 from wounds received in action on the 9 Sept 1916.	S.

11/9/16
12/9/16
13/9/16

SECRET

WAR DIARY
or
INTELLIGENCE SUMMARY

(Erase heading not required.)

Army Form C. 2118

of 6th (S) Bn The Royal Scots Regt
Pp 1 & 2 & 3
September 1916.

Place	Date	Hour	Summary of Events and Information	Remarks and references to Appendices
VAUX	14/9/16		Major H.J. TAYLOR from the D.L.I (51st DIV) assumed command of the Bn from Lt Colr. CAPT A.D. PEARCE M.C. granted M.C. Brigade Comnd. at 8 p.m. at B/de H.Q.	R.
"	15/9/16		The Bn moved into camp on VAUX-CORBIE road. Bn moved off at 2 p.m. The 6th Bn was billetted at Right & left jumps.	R.
"	17/9/16		Transport Brigaded together moved to LA CHAUSSEE en route for HUPPY	R.
HUPPY	18/9/16		The 6th Royal Scots moved to HUPPY en motor lorries, leaving at 10 a.m. and arriving at HUPPY at 7.30 p.m.	R.
	20/9/16		The D.O. made orders to move to ABBEVILLE for entraining.	R.
	21/9/16		The 6th Royal Scots paraded at 2.45 a.m. and marched to ABBEVILLE where they entrained with transport for BAILLEUL, arriving at that place at 3.15 p.m. and marched to billets about 2 miles EAST of FLETRE & South WEST of BAILLEUL.	R.
	24/9/16		At 8 a.m. The Bn paraded and marched in Brigade to hutted camp (M.G.D.6.) on KEMMEL-POPERINGHE road.	R.

Army Form C. 2118

WAR DIARY
or
INTELLIGENCE SUMMARY

SECRET of 6th (S) Bn. The Royal Irish Regt. Sheet 4.
September 1916

(Erase heading not required.)

Place	Date	Hour	Summary of Events and Information	Remarks and references to Appendices
M.6.D.6.7	25/9/16		The Army Commander inspected the 6th Royal Irish Regt at Bde. H.Q. 5 Officers & 22 men joined this day.	A.S.
	27/9/16		The Bde. moved into their new line of trenches, the 6th Royal Irish Regt. remaining at M.6.D.6.7. in Bde. Reserve.	A.S.
	30/9/16		The Comdg. Officer proceeded to ENGLAND on special leave for 10 days. This closes the WAR DIARY for the month of SEPTEMBER 1916.	A.S.

E.E. Marsh Capt. Comdg.
6th Royal Irish Regt.

WAR DIARY

MONTH OF OCTOBER, 1916.

VOLUME

6th Royal Irish Regiment.

WAR DIARY of 2/6 R(S) Bn. Royal Scots Regt.

INTELLIGENCE SUMMARY

Sheet I.

October 1916

Place	Date	Hour	Summary of Events and Information	Remarks and references to Appendices
LACLYTTE	1st		The Bn. shelled. Div: Reserve at M.G.D. Camp. Lt. PHILLIPS joined for duty. A draft of 63 O.R. arrived & were posted to coys.	15.
SIEGE Fm.	5th		The Bn. relieved the 6th CONNAUGHT RANGERS in support to the firing line. H.Q. at SIEGE Fm.	15.
"	6th		CAPT MARSH ordered to take charge of DIV. Drainage Coy	15.
YORK HOUSE	9th		The Bn. relieved the 7th LEINSTERS in firing line with H.Q. at YORK HOUSE. Trenches shelled by hostile MINENWERFERS, no casualties. A damage caused on detonation.	15.
"	11th		Own artillery fired slow today, but caused no casualties. Our own T.M. 36th DIV. ARTY. was relieved by the 16th DIV. ARTY. Own artillery been very slow & half-hearted in activity with T.M.s.	15.
"	12th		Heavy hostile activity of T.M.S. Own artillery been very slow & half-hearted in giving retaliation.	15.
BUTTERFLY Fm.	13th		The Bn. was relieved by the 6th CONNAUGHT RANGERS & moved into B. of Reserve at BUTTERFLY Fm. Total casualties during tour = 10. R. wounded.	15.
"	15th		Two drivers P/o FRIEL & M/Cann returned at 9.25 a.m.	15.
"	17th		9/47 LARACY joined for duty. (height 6'7" in his socks)	15.

664d

SECRET

Army Form C. 2118

WAR DIARY or INTELLIGENCE SUMMARY

of The Royal Irish Regt.

(Erase heading not required.) 6 October 1916.

Place	Date	Hour	Summary of Events and Information	Remarks and references to Appendices
BUTTERFLY FM	19th		Pte FRIEL & McCANN tried by F.G.C.M. & sentenced to 5 years commutes imprisonment with H.L. commuted to 90 days F.P.N°1	
SIEGE FM	21st		Bn. moved into billets at 6th CONNAUGHT RANGERS SIEGE FM	
YORK HOUSE	25th		Bn. moved into billets having been relieved by 7th LEINSTERS. Bombers trained in STOKES Bomb. Remainder in 2 platoon squads 10 R killed & 10 R wounded of ration party. Enemy patrol entered 3 or 4 empty bombing posts & effectively bombed. Other posts were empty. Enemy has very strong patrols in No man's land & are active with good patrolling. No man's land to our front contains no dead & should yield good patrolling from Enemy.	
" "	26th		2 R. left effective for duty. 2 men killed & 6 wounded & 1 gas conference. Seven Officers and 1 N.C.O. joined for duty.	
" "	28th		Bn. in front line. 6th CONNAUGHT RANGERS sent 4 R. in MCD	
MCD & LACLYTTE	29th		Bn. was relieved by 6th CONNAUGHT RANGERS & proceeded to CLYTTE CAMP (M.60) temporarily with 49th Bde on our right. Bn. eventually relieved and G.O.C. 49th Bde. commanding in same thro (?)	
" "	31st		LT COL H.J. TAYLOR ordered to take command of 17th (S.) WELSH FUS. & proceed to join them. He assumed command & the 6th ROYAL IRISH on march of 24 oct ROY E. KELLY 1st Bn. The ROYAL IRISH P.S.C. started the WAR DIARY for the month of OCTOBER 1916	

Signed

Lieut. Colonel,
Comd'g 6th. (Ser.) Bn: The Royal Irish Regt.

WAR   DIARY.

FOR

MONTH   OF   NOVEMBER,   1916.

VOLUME   12.

6th R. Irish Regiment

WAR DIARY or INTELLIGENCE SUMMARY

Army Form C. 2118

of J.H.(S) B⁻ 7th Royal Irish Reg⁻ November 1916

Place	Date	Hour	Summary of Events and Information	Remarks and references to Appendices
CURRAGH CAMP	1st		The Battalion moved from M6d and the new Recruit Camp & he called in future "The CURRAGH CAMP." food accommodation is to be & rent on strong Battalion.	
"	4th		Visit to this area by the DUKE OF CONNAUGHT. dismounted as usual for inspection. Carried out to be bought on to Afternoon. 2/Lt S.M. WOLF found the day for duty with & Battalion	
SIEGE FM	6th		The Battalion this day marched out before & to meet the 5th MUNSTERS, RANGERS and SIEGE FM, KILMER of strong front. The O.C.2/Lt ROSS MUNSTER FUSILIERS carried out a raid, mostly Summer and. was and successful on enemy establishment.	
"	7th		2/Lt HALL to hospital with influenza; Say they were all off. SIEG AM. for bombing work later.	
"	8th		The 47 k Brit Defence scheme carried on as a Regiment exercise weather right my good.	
"	9th		A great conference on this weather 2/Lt SLATER & has assumed command of B.Coy. 2/Lt GOWTHORPE appointed assistant adjutant.	

Army Form C. 2118

WAR DIARY
or
INTELLIGENCE SUMMARY J R 6 R(S) 1 n
The Royal Irish Rg.
November 1916

(Erase heading not required.)

SECRET
Sheet II

Instructions regarding War Diaries and Intelligence Summaries are contained in F.S. Regs., Part II. and the Staff Manual respectively. Title Pages will be prepared in manuscript.

Place	Date	Hour	Summary of Events and Information	Remarks and references to Appendices
YORK HOUSE	10th		The Battalion moved into the front line & VAN KEEP & relieved the 7th LEINSTER REGT. Draft of 50 O.R. joined this day. The division on our left carried out a bombardment of enemy's trenches & inspected trench-mortars emplacements. Lt DILLON to hospital with jaundice	K
"	11th		A draft of 111 O.R. joined this day. 2/Lt. COGAN returned from a course of general instruction at WISQUES.	K
"	12th		2/Lt. PEMBERTON & 2/Lt. STOKER reported from the command school this day.	K
"	13th		Mortar activity by their trench mortars, especially on VAN KEEP. Enemy reported this day and I regret to add that CAPT. PHILLIPS & 1 O.R. were killed and 2 O.R. wounded.	K
"	14th		The Battalion, relieved this day by the 6th CONNAUGHT RANGERS, moved into brigade support at BUTTERFLY FM. CAPT PHILLIPS was this day at KEMMEL cemetery. CPL RICHER buried at the MILITARY CEMETERY, near YORK HOUSE.	K

WAR DIARY / INTELLIGENCE SUMMARY

Army Form C. 2118

SECRET

Instructions regarding War Diaries and Intelligence Summaries are contained in F.S. Regs., Part II. and the Staff Manual respectively. Title Pages will be prepared in manuscript.

(Erase heading not required.)

of the 6th (S.) Bn. The Royal Sussex Regt.

November 1916

Place	Date	Hour	Summary of Events and Information	Remarks and references to Appendices
BOTTERFLYER	15th		The 47th Bde Defence scheme was carried out as a Bde Ve exercise	
"	17th		The Bn Major was allotted to the Bde by an WESTOUTRE	
"	19th		A draft of 28 O.R. joined the Bn	
"	20th		5 Bn officers Reg B team played against the 7th LEINSTERS & were beaten 2-4 Front to nil. Canadian Bn officers rumoured not men only	
"	21st		A draft of 61 O.R. joined this Bn, composed again mostly of old soldiers who joined C.Q.M. Sergeants amongst them	
"	22nd		The Battalion moved out & relieved the 6 Cameront RANGERS	
SIEGE FM	24th		A draft of 58 O.R. joined the Bn, composed mostly of Sythonian taken from the supplies R.F.A. recruits from the line travel. Nones to Rontraye did but little damage. Bn in relation through 2 Coys was excellent	

SECRET

Army Form C. 2118

Instructions regarding War Diaries and Intelligence Summaries are contained in F.S. Regs., Part II. and the Staff Manual respectively. Title Pages will be prepared in manuscript.

WAR DIARY
or
INTELLIGENCE SUMMARY

(Erase heading not required.)

of the 6(S) Bn. or the Royal Irish Regt.
November 1916.

Place	Date	Hour	Summary of Events and Information	Remarks and references to Appendices
SIEG.E	PM 25		At dark 4 O.R. joined this day. Weather bad with heavy rain.	
YORK HOUSE	26		The Battalion relieved the 7th Leinsters in the front line YUAN ROS.P. MAYO STREET bombarded with aerial darts, 2 O.R. killed & 4 wounded.	
"	" 27		MAYO STREET again bombarded with aerial darts, by the same of the same? hence to a msg, 2.O.R. killed.	
"	" 29		A strong patrol went out under Capt DAY & 2/Lt WOOD to get a prisoner, as patrols discovered of ours moved to flank to get through. Two cotton was placed under the enemy's wire & a dummy raid carried out with the help of the artillery. The patrol returned safely at 1.15 a.m. when the enemy rapidly opened fire.	
"	" 30		Enemy did some damage to the barrier as all to try we wire bombarded. Several mortars & aerial darts without causing any material damage. 5th R.I.R. was relieved 1st O.B. by 1st R.R.ROYAL MUNSTER FUSILIERS & went into divisional reserve at CURRAGH CAMP. This closes the war diary for the month of November 1916.	

[signed] Comd'g 6th. (Ser.S) Bn. The Royal Irish Regt.

WAR DIARY FOR MONTH OF DECEMBER, 1916.

VOLUME 13.

6th R Irish Regiment

WAR DIARY
or
INTELLIGENCE SUMMARY

of the 6th Royal Irish Regt
December 1916   Sheet 15

Army Form C. 2118

Place	Date	Hour	Summary of Events and Information	Remarks and references to Appendices
CURRAGH CAMP	1-12-16		Lt Col Roche-Kelly on leave to England. General de Lusier Protard inspected the	
"	2-12-16		Kied by 41st Division 3 prisoners captured. Gas blown at mid-night but nothing doing	
"	5-12-16		7 Mines for leave	
"	8-12-16		Capt Hutcheson joined for duty	
"	9-12-16		2Lt Jaines & 11 O.R. joined	
"	10-12-16		Draft of 46 O.R. joined	
"	11-12-16		Capt Ward-Simpson to Brigade for instruction as Staff Captain. 2Lt Gonthorpe that over duties as Adjt.	
COOKER FARM	12-12-16		Relieved the 6th Connaught Rangers in new line	
"	13-12-16		Between the hours of 2pm & 4pm our T.M's & Stokes were very active. The enemy retaliated but caused very little damage. One man wounded	
"	14-12-16		In reply to our Stokes enemy established with T.M's & shrapnel. Considerable damage was caused in our front line but no casualties	
"	15-12-16		T.M's active all day but very little damage caused. 1000 YDR joined. 2Lt Salmon left on leave	

WAR DIARY or INTELLIGENCE SUMMARY

Army Form C. 2118

1st Royal Irish Regt

November 1916

SHEET No.

Place	Date	Hour	Summary of Events and Information	Remarks and references to Appendices
COOKER FARM	16-11-16		At noon the enemy shelled our Lewis Gun Position who were by H.Q. Three direct hits were obtained on the M.D.S. which killed one man & wounded eighteen. Our T.M's were very active during the afternoon.	
"	17-11-16	2.30pm	Our T.M's & Stokes fired on enemy front line. Enemy retaliated but caused very little damage. Two men killed.	
"	18-11-16	2.30pm	Our T.M's & Stokes opened but received no retaliation. Enemy whistling and gas alarm.	
"	19-11-16		Staff of 1st D.R. joined	
"	20-11-16		Relieved by 6th C.R. moved to DERRY HUTS. Left dry — left on time.	
DERRY HUTS	24-11-16		Bde S.O.S. test alarm. The Battn. ready to move in 30 minutes.	
"	25-11-16		X.M.A.S. dinners	
"	26-11-16		2 Lt Dunne left on leave	
"	28-11-16		Relieved 6 G.C.R. 2 Lt Turner returned from leave	
COOKER FARM	29-11-16		Enemy shelled a few shells along SPUD ROAD	

Army Form C. 2118
SHEET 17

WAR DIARY 6th Royal Irish Regt
or
INTELLIGENCE SUMMARY December 1916

(Erase heading not required.)

Place	Date	Hour	Summary of Events and Information	Remarks and references to Appendices
COOKER FARM	30-12-16		Enemy Artillery more active than usual	
"	31-12-16		Lt RENNISON reported Missing believed killed. 2 Coys left on leave drafts of 48 O.R.	

E J Kelly
Lieut. Colonel.
Comd'g 8th (Ser.) Bn. The Royal Irish Regt.

31 DEC 1916

WAR DIARY for month of JANUARY, 1917.

VOLUME 14

6th Royal Irish Regiment

Army Form C. 2118.

WAR DIARY
or
INTELLIGENCE SUMMARY.

(Erase heading not required.)

6th Royal Irish Regt
January 1917 [sic?] 18

Place	Date	Hour	Summary of Events and Information	Remarks and references to Appendices
COOKER FARM	1-1-17		Our Artillery active all day. Half day received off duty. The O.C. of Bgde & S.C. at Manor held a Tug of War stakes. Enemy retaliated on our arties shots but not very little damage	
"	2-1-17		Enemy's artillery active all day. SHAMUS FARM and S.P.'s heavy shelled all round "Middle" on "Hilltop" & also BAYONET CORNER	
"	3-1-17		During the day enemy retaliated on CANADA CORNER	
"	4-1-17		Relieved by 2nd R. MUNSTER FUS. Went to CANADA CORNER	
FERRAGH CAMP	5-1-17		2/Lt WALL 2.S.R. left us on being transferred to half. 25-R. Left to join 142 or 72 Coy RE	
"	9-1-17		Lts MARTIN & DICKSON on leave	
"	10-1-17		Lt Collet the 8 1/D CAVALIERS	
"	13-1-17		Capt Holl & Lt McCUTCHEON on leave	
COOKER FARM	15-1-17		Our TM's & STOKES acted fairly now & then. TM's on front line 4.2 on S.P's.	
"	16-1-17		Enemy opened with TM's on front line 4.2 on S.P.G.	
"	17-1-17		Our TM's & STOKES were again active during the morning & afternoon. Lt remained on retaliation	
"	18-1-17		2/Lt TOOMEY killed by a strike	

WAR DIARY
or
INTELLIGENCE SUMMARY.
(Erase heading not required.)

Army Form C. 2118.

6th Royal Irish Regt

January 1917 SHEET 17

Place	Date	Hour	Summary of Events and Information	Remarks and references to Appendices
COOKER FARM	19-1-17		Enemy T.M.s were active during the day but were replied to	
"	19-1-17		2Lt Tydd wounded 1 O.R. killed	
"	20-1-17		Mr Bar and T.M. Stokes Battery opened on enemy and did considerable damage	
"	21-1-17		The relation carried out to-day by the 6 R. Chargers	
DERRY HUTS	28-1-17		We were relieved by the 6 R. Chargers	
COOKER FARM	27-1-17		Enemy sent over a few T.Ms at 2 p.m. but nothing doing	
"	28-1-17		We had a bombard battery. The day's about & of their shells	
"			"Duchess" also assisted. Retaliation on our batteries was very heavy	
"	29-1-17		with 4.2 H.E. but very little damage was done	
"			We were relieved by the 7th Leinsters front & support Battns & proceeded	
DERRY HUTS	30-1-17		to DERRY HUTS	
"	31-1-17			

[signature]

Comdg 6th (Ser.) Bn. The Royal Irish Regt

[stamp: ORDERLY ROOM 2 FEB 1917 6th (Ser) Bn. The Royal Irish Regt]

WAR DIARY.

FOR MONTH OF FEBRUARY, 1917.

VOLUME 15

UNIT:- 6th Royal Irish Regiment.

SECRET

Army Form C. 2118.

WAR DIARY of 6th (S) Batt. Royal Irish
INTELLIGENCE SUMMARY. Regt. February 1917

(Erase heading not required.)

Place	Date	Hour	Summary of Events and Information	Remarks and references to Appendices
DERRY HTS	1st		About 5 a.m. Enemy's bombardment commenced & H.A. was ordered to stand to. At the enemy's own shelling with gas shells a battery in the ground of the Boyd's Stables drawn heck but concealed Gas Batteries area camp heavily shelled all morning.	B.
	2nd		The Battalion relieved the 6th Connaught Rangers in front line of the new left subsection (N. of Piccadilly to Broadway). HQ. at FORT VICTORIA	B.
FORT VICTORIA	3rd		Very quiet except for good actions of hostile aeroplanes.	
" "	4th		Lt. Col. E. ROCHE-KELLY, took over 2nd Army course, Draman command of B. the Bn. All leave cancelled.	
" "	5th		Enemy bombarded our centre front line until T.M.S.Y 5.30, as counter enemy B. with damage done.	
" "	6th		The 7th Inniskillings relieved the Bn & Bn moved into DONCASTER HORSE.	B.

SECRET

Army Form C. 2118.

Instructions regarding War Diaries and Intelligence
Summaries are contained in F. S. Regs., Part II.
and the Staff Manual respectively. Title pages
will be prepared in manuscript.

WAR DIARY
or
INTELLIGENCE SUMMARY.
(Erase heading not required.)

6/14(S) 03 Th Royal Irish Regt Sheet 77
February 1916

Place	Date	Hour	Summary of Events and Information	Remarks and references to Appendices
DONCASTER HUTS	7th		Reconnaissance of Assembly positions to be taken up in case of attack. North Liphan Av. at 9.14 a.m. An archie fell just near H.Q. more hutting has been belongs to 16th Canl 48th INF. BDE.	
"	10th		A/G.O.C. 16th DIV. inspected the huts in the afternoon. Certain repairs to be carried out immediately. Enemy aeroplanes active most of the day.	
"	12th		Cross country for the whole B'n. Distance about 7000 yds. Won by Pte BURNS C.Cy. Major HUTCHESSON a very good 14th, very keen going all the way.	
"	13th		Bathing of whole Battalion in morning. Very good lectures in Sparkford in even'g. Emptire. O.C. Col. MOORE D.S.O. & of the CINEMA	
"	14th		Probably for the first time in history the 6th B'n relieved the 2nd Rl Irish 18th H in the in support to the left subsection H.Q. DOCTORS HOUSE Brother hun fine.	

SECRET

Army Form C. 2118.

WAR DIARY
of 2/L(S) Co 7th Royal Irish Rifles
INTELLIGENCE SUMMARY.
(Erase heading not required.)

Sheet II

Instructions regarding War Diaries and Intelligence Summaries are contained in F. S. Regs., Part II. and the Staff Manual respectively. Title pages will be prepared in manuscript.

Place	Date	Hour	Summary of Events and Information	Remarks and references to Appendices
DOCTORS H₉	15th		Enemy hand killed field battery on KEMMEL SIEGE 5 PM over night 5 P.I. & asphyxiating shells. Three or four S.G's landed close to H.Q. no shells or damage to KEMMEL CHATEAU, adm. casualties.	
"	16th		Commencement of Cops artillery bombardment. Very little retaliation on our F.S. trench.	
"	17th		At four S.G's landed near DOCTORS HOUSE, Cops being artillery bombardment F.S. at 10.45 a.m. & 1.30 p.m.	
F.T. VICTORIA	18th		The Bn. relieved the 6/ I.C.R. on front line of F.S. relieved in H.Q. at F.T. VICTORIA. Another bombardment of Cops. 1 Lad & man 3 O.R. wounded.	
"	19th		Raid by 6 I.C.R. accompanied by discharge of gas at 3.15 a.m. 15N a success. Germans heftet to open our wounded on NO MAN'S LAND. 10 O.R. & 2 male Lewis S/ MORRISSEY man died of wounds. Arrived in LOCRE.	

T2134. Wt. W708-776. 50C000. 4/15. Sir J. C. & S.

SECRET

Army Form C. 2118.

WAR DIARY
or
INTELLIGENCE SUMMARY. 6 ᵗʰ (S) & 7ᵗʰ Royal Irish Regt.

(Erase heading not required.)

Sheet IV

Instructions regarding War Diaries and Intelligence Summaries are contained in F.S. Regs., Part II. and the Staff Manual respectively. Title pages will be prepared in manuscript.

Place	Date	Hour	Summary of Events and Information	Remarks and references to Appendices
FT. VICTORIA	20ᵗʰ		Conference of Bⁿ Commanders at Bⁿ H.Q. Another bombardment of bay expected. Arrival of the DIV. ARTY. Rained all afternoon.	15
"	21ˢᵗ		Heavy artillery again bombarded both had area. Enemy answers a few shrap-bangs on A Coy H.Q. (W.A. GELLIS)	15
"	22ⁿᵈ		2/Lt. JOHNSTON wounded on the Coy short (eye injury). Total casualties during tour in the trenches 2.O.R. killed, 1 Off & 9 O.R. wounded. The Bⁿ was relieved at 5 pm by the 2ᵗʰ INNIS. FUS. The Bⁿ marched into DONCASTER CAMP.	15
DONCASTER	24ᵗʰ		The A/G.O.C. inspected Contents Q. for 2ⁿᵈ Army & shot me out [illeg] 1.O.R. very smart turn-out.	15
"	26ᵗʰ		Inspection by G.O.C. Informal general approval of the C.O. of the turn-out & smartness of all ranks on parade.	15
"	27ᵗʰ		CAPT. O'BRIEN-BUTLER E.A./admit K.A.2. Lt. JORDAN BENSELAND fr. interview for commission in the INDIAN ARMY. This closes the War Diary for month of February.	15

E. John O'Hill

WAR DIARY

FOR MONTH OF MARCH, 1917.

VOLUME 16

UNIT:- 6th Btn Royal Irish Regiment.

'SECRET'

Army Form C. 2118.

Instructions regarding War Diaries and Intelligence Summaries are contained in F.S. Regs. Part II. and the Staff Manual respectively. Title pages will be prepared in manuscript.

WAR DIARY
or
INTELLIGENCE SUMMARY.
(Erase heading not required.)

of the 6/Royal Irish Fus Bn Rud I
March 1917.

Place	Date	Hour	Summary of Events and Information	Remarks and references to Appendices
DONCASTER HUTS.	1st		Draft of 31 O.R arrived. Reg'tl. 00's v when match against 7/LEINSTERS won by 10 goals to nil.	1S
F.VICTORIA	2nd		Relieved the 7th R. INNIS. FUS. on the left subsector.	R
	4th		Demonstration of Barrage (creeping) by Div Arty on SPANBROEK MOLEN, no hostile retaliation.	1S
	5th		Reinforcement of Div Arty and 7.15 a.m. slight retaliation no casualties.	1S
	6th		Relieved by the 6 CONNAUGHT RANGERS and moved out one coy supported at DERRY HUTS. (2 b casualties during this tour.	1S
	7th		CAPT O'BRIEN-BUTLER 1/R LEINS VIERSTRAAT for three day attachment to the R.F.A. (A/150 S.I.Y.)	R
	8th		Germans raided 4SSLN & 71 Des about 4.30 p.m. B2 did not now stand-to as the wind was Eastry. Eastwards & nothing unusual reported to be happening.	1S
	9th		At 4.30 a.m. The S.O.S came from the B2 on right subsector and the 6/R.I. Fus did 1S
6b. Normal in came through about 5.15 am and it S.O. stood down with the hands of	1S
			close to DERRY HUTS.	
F.VICTORIA	10th		Relieved the 6/CONNAUGHT RANGERS on the Lone Ruis, a big Jap on GEORGES HOLE HANTS PIONEERS dined in good for the round in reg Pt.	1S

T2134. Wt. W708-776. 50C000. 4/15. Sir J.C. & S.

Army Form C. 2118

WAR DIARY
or
INTELLIGENCE SUMMARY

(Erase heading not required.)

The 6th Royal Irish Rgt
Sheet 2
March 1917

Place	Date	Hour	Summary of Events and Information	Remarks and references to Appendices
Ft VICTORIA	12th		2/Lt. HEWITT wounded on duty whilst on patrol.	15
	13th		2/Lt. LORACY slightly wounded on the leg (was taken off) otherwise on way from patrol.	15
DOCTOR'S HOUSE			Relieved by 10th Royal Irish Rifles (36th Div.) and moved into our Rgt's BERTHEN AREA, arriving about 9.30 p.m.	15
	14th		Relieved by the 8th Royal Irish Rifles at 6 a.m. and marched to BERTHEN AREA, arriving about 9.30 p.m.	15
BERTHEN	15th		Conference of Comdg. Officers at ADC. H.Q. (THIEUSHOUK) at 5.30 p.m. Hon Lt & Qm. REGAN proceeds on leave not ferried it.	15
"	16th		2/Lts BURKE and LAMB reported. Draft of 23 other ranks ordered it 6 recruits joined this day.	15
"	17th		ST. PATRICK'S DAY. Church Parade & the C.O. spoke. News arrived of the capture of BAPAUME e.t.c.	15
"	18th		Train for R.C.'s cancelled. Lt. Col. Lefroy at WESTOUTRE.	16
"	19th		The Comdg. Off. proceeds on leave until April 9. Lt. Boyle But CHESSON assumed command of the Bn.	15

SECRET

Instructions regarding War Diaries and Intelligence Summaries are contained in F.S. Regs., Part II and the Staff Manual respectively. Title Pages will be prepared in manuscript.

WAR DIARY
or
INTELLIGENCE SUMMARY

(Erase heading not required.)

Army Form C. 2118

1st Th. 6/Royal East Reg.
Sheet 3.

March 1917

Place	Date	Hour	Summary of Events and Information	Remarks and references to Appendices
BERTHEN AREA	20th		B.H. Sports held all day. 2/Lt PATMAN reports from Grenade Course (excellent report, passed as qualified Instructor).	A.
" "	21st		Ceremonial parade in preparation of The Army Commander's visit. 1st class of 25 O.R. joined this day.	A.
" "	22nd		The inspection by the Army Commander at 11.45 a.m. Very satisfactory. 2/Lt. GOWTHORPE reports from a course with the R.F.C. CAPT TAYLOR to be attached to 2nd H.Q.	A.
" "	23rd		2nd class of 12 O.R. joined. Practice of the new organization.	A.
" "	25th		CAPT TAYLOR transferred to the 2nd ROYAL IRISH REGT.	A.
" "	26th		CAPT. FRANKENBORG to hospital with German measles.	A.
" "	27th		CAPT O'BRIEN-BUTLER to hospital (head-sores). 2/Lt ONSOWE to be attached to 1st Bn. R.I.R. ew BOESCHEPE AREA. 2/LT CROWE to be attached also for R. GOWTHORPE who takes up the duties of gun catcher for the whole R.I. 2/LT. V. HUNTER joins from Y.D. AZ.	A.

1875 Wt. W593/826 1,000,000 4/15 J.B.C. & A. A.D.S.S./Forms/C. 2118.

WAR DIARY
or
INTELLIGENCE SUMMARY

Army Form C. 2118

6th Royal Irish Regt.
March 1917

Place	Date	Hour	Summary of Events and Information	Remarks and references to Appendices
BERTHEN AREA	27/5 cont.		2/Lt JORDAN & the signalling officer and 2/Lt JOHNSTON & embarkation wounded, & charge of 3.O.R. joined today.	K
" "	29th		CAPT. LEA-WILSON joined today. B Coy. have been behind back up to 15.	
" "	31st		The Bn. moved at 9.30 a.m. into the LOCRE AREA & relieved the 2nd R. DUB. FUS.	R
			KEMMEL SHELTERS, relieving the 2nd R. DUB. FUS.
This ends the War Diary for the month of March 1917.	

J.J.W.Wynter Major
Comm'g 6th (Serv) Bn The Royal Irish Regt.

WAR DIARY FOR MONTH OF APRIL, 1917.

VOLUME:- 14

UNIT:- 6th R. Irish Regiment

WAR DIARY / INTELLIGENCE SUMMARY

Army Form C. 2118

6th Royal Irish Regt.

April 1917

Sheet 1.

Place	Date	Hour	Summary of Events and Information	Remarks and references to Appendices
KEMMEL SHELTERS Right Subsection WYTSCHAETE SECTOR.	1st		Relieved the 2nd Royal Irish in the Right Subsection. 2 Coys in the line, 2 in support, H.Q. at TURVER REDOUBT. Fairly quiet night.	
Right Subsection WYTSCHAETE SECTOR.	2nd		Sgt. DONNAN wounded in the hand. 1 O.R. killed. Snowing heavily most of 24 hours. 1st Lt BLAVEY injured from Grenade Case.	
"	3rd		Snowed hard all night, practically no patrols possible. From 5.30 to 6.40 p.m. "X" day bombardment put the forthcoming raid on 5th. Very little retaliation	
"	4th		"Y" day Bombardment from 5.30 p.m. to 6.40 p.m. Large amount of retaliation, the enemy putting up a Box barrage down ROSSIGNOL ROAD also PARK St. and up VIA GELIA, extremely accurate. No casualties with the Battalion. T.M. Battery had 1 O.R. killed.	
" to BUTTERFLY FARM.	5th		"Z" day. The RAID. A most successful undertaking, 21 prisoners 9th Grenadier Regt. (wounded) 2/Lt. R.Z.G. Barker (wounded) - Capt. T.E. Day (died of wounds), Lieut. Williams information was gained. Casualties :- Capt. T.E. Day (died of wounds), Lieut. Williams 6 killed. 7 missing. 66 wounded. While Battalion quietly slated at our great success. Relieved by 6th Connaught Rangers at 2.12 a.m. & moved to Brigade support at BUTTERFLY FARM.	
BUTTERFLY FARM.	6th		Major General Hickie comdg. 16th Division visited the Battalion to congratulate. Congratulations also received from 2/Army Commander, 49th Brigade.	

WAR DIARY
INTELLIGENCE SUMMARY

(Erase heading not required.)

Army Form C. 2118

6th Royal Irish Regt.
April 1917
Sheet II.

Place	Date	Hour	Summary of Events and Information	Remarks and references to Appendices
BUTTERFLY FARM.	7th.		Baths for the Battalion. Funeral of Capt. Day in BAILEUL. Many spoke on the Divisional area.	Appx.
"	8th.		2/Lt about & C.in.C; Probably a raid. Easter Sunday. Church Parade. Memorial Service for Capt. Day.	Appx.
"	9th.		General clean up for Army Commanders inspection.	Appx.
"	10th.		Inspected by Army Commander at 11.30 a.m, in a field near LOCRE, he was very pleased and ordered the parade. All arms fatigue Party in the road were represented. Relieved 6th Connaught Rangers in the line Right Subsector WYTSCHAETE	Appx.
Right Subsection WYTSCHAETE	11th.		2/Lt. Robinson from Leave, great reconnaissance. "Big Push" down South.	Appx.
"	12th.		Our T.M.s did new wire cutting near PETIT BOIS.	Appx.
"	13th.		2/Lt HEWITT to Transport. Heavy bombard hostile trenches all day from 9am to 3pm. Wire cutting by T.M.s at PETIT BOIS.	Appx.
"	14th.		New wire cutting at PETIT BOIS. 5 p.m. to 9 a.m T.M.s. Two enemy aeroplanes flew over very low about 9-45am and dropped white lights.	Appx.
"	15th.		Bombardment of hostile trenches A.M heavier; relieved by 6th Connaught Rangers & move into Brigade Support at ROSSIGNOL ESTAMINET.	Appx.
ROSSIGNOL ESTAMINET	16th.		Quiet day. Battalion very scattered as regards billets.	Appx.
"	17th.		Weather bad. Working parties supplied in large numbers.	Appx.
"	18th.		Very quiet day. Heavy fatigues for the men.	Appx.
"	19th.		Relieved by 9th Royal Dublin Fusiliers; move to KEMMEL SHELTERS.	Appx.

Army Form C. 2118

WAR DIARY or ~~INTELLIGENCE SUMMARY~~

(Erase heading not required.)

6th Royal Irish Regt.

April 1917

Sheet III

Place	Date	Hour	Summary of Events and Information	Remarks and references to Appendices
KEMMEL SHELTERS	20th		2/Lt Lamb rejoins. 2/Lt Barry wounded on working party. Heavy shell by KEMMEL.	WD
"	21st		Major Mitchelson on leave. Capt. V.E. Ward-Simpson On a course. Capt. O'Brien Butler 2nd in Command.	WD
"	22nd		Working parties found slightly. Relations of officers Batts.	WD
"	23rd		Training carried out strenuously by all ranks.	WD
"	24th		Very heavy bombardment up North about 10.P.M. Prepare to move to CLARE CAMP.	WD
CLARE CAMP	25th		Left KEMMEL SHELTERS for CLARE CAMP. Very poor accommodation at this Camp.	WD
"	26th		Brigade Training ground not too good. The Battalion good use being made of Company training.	WD
"	27th		Company training and route marches.	WD
"	28th		2/Lt Leahy joined. Football match with R.F.C. 7th Battalion won 2-1. Divisional Concert performed in CLARE CAMP.	WD
"	29th		Moves to CAESTRE cancelled. Holiday, great aerial activity.	WD
"	30th		Practice at Rifle firing. Two men O'Brien due to join Company training and route marches.	WD

This ends the War Diary for the month of April 1917.

Signed J. O'Brien Butler Capt.
6th (Ser) Battn. Royal Irish Regt.
Commander
6th (Ser) Battn. Royal Irish Regt.

W A R   D I A R Y :
-----------oOo-----------

VOLUME:- 18

FOR MONTH OF MAY, 1917.

UNIT:- 6th R. Irish Regiment

WAR DIARY or INTELLIGENCE SUMMARY

Army Form C. 2118

6th Royal Irish Rgt.
May 1917.
Sheet I

Place	Date	Hour	Summary of Events and Information	Remarks and references to Appendices
CLARE CAMP.	1st		rejoined Capt Shanahan & 157 [?] rejoined. Enemy aircraft very busy during the morning. Battalion started in the afternoon must have excited[?] [?] enemy[?] firing[?] on account of their keeping close enough to it. Range at LOCRE HOSPICE at disposal of Battalion. Attack practice in the afternoon.	
"	2nd			
"	3rd		Training granted at dispersal Battalion. Demonstration in Brigade Training ground of Fg. B.M. & [?] consolidating a Strong Point.	
"	4th		Shots[?] 157 & R.2. Attack Practice. Three enemy aeroplanes over.	
"	5th		Relief 9th Royal Dublin Fusiliers in the night Subsection WYTSCHAETE. Weather very warm. One of our aeroplanes came down shot down in our lines BEAVER FARM return fire by Hostile Shelling.	
Rg(U)Subsector WYTSCHAETE	6th		Capt Saylor to LE TOUQUET on g. H.Q. Lewis gun course. Very slight artillery activity.	
"	7th		In punishment to hostile shelling I both our and Hostiles bombarded the enemy lines to fire minimiz firing standingping any note.	
"	8th		Enemy heavily shelled battery positions during the day.	
"	9th		Night: 9th/10th a small enterprise was carried out, 2/Lt Dunne & 9 Dunne[?] with 25 men entered the enemy lines in the PETIT BOIS Salient and arrived at Dunne (strip) Mission three men killed two men [?] accounted for. Two men [?] wounded and three others wounded. Division 33rd Infantry Regiment 2nd Division.	

WAR DIARY

Army Form C. 2118

1st Royal Irish Regt.
Sheet II
Nov 1917.

Place	Date	Hour	Summary of Events and Information	Remarks and references to Appendices
CARNARVON CAMP ST.SYLVESTRE CAPPEL.	10th		Relieved by 2nd Royal Irish Regt. March to CARNARVON CAMP. Made the Building our EECKE - ST SYLVESTRE CAPPEL. Capt Franhurberger ??? T	
"	11th		Several clean up. This weather men sheltering at Church Parade. Draft of 13 O.Rs arrived. Conference at Brigade H.Q.	
"	12th		Draft of 30 O.Rs arrived.	
"	13th			
"	14th		Preparation for the march. General clean up.	
"	15th		Reconnaissance & Training area billeting at EBBLINGHEM, for the night. Route via	
EBBLINGHEM WIZERNES.	16th		HAZEBROUCK march. Spent the night at WIZERNES. Route via FORT ROUGE. Number of	
"	17th		Performance march. Sprinting the men with the great care approximation the morning.	
ALQUINES	18th		March to ALQUINES. Very hot weather. Billets very good for all ranges. Start laying out a copy of the country.	
"	19th		Conference at Brigade Training ground, Specifying the great for the practice attack.	
"	20th		BWYTSCHAETE - Good progress being made. Our Battalion does a practice attack. Companies. Training of Specialists & Battalion Training great used by Companies.	
"	21st			
"	22nd		The Battalion does another preliminary practice attack on the Brigade ground.	
"	23rd		Battalion Training ground ready for companies. Training of specialists. Lecture from R.F.C. Lt He with again from Lewis, Lewis, Mills	
"	24th		LYTTON given H.Y. & SHAFTE Lecture was completed till Brigade till Dog. Quite satisfactory.	
"	25th		Great Brigade Field Day, hot satisfactory. A Civilian shot by a man the Battalion.	

WAR DIARY
INTELLIGENCE SUMMARY

Army Form C. 2118.

7th Royal Irish Regt.
6th (Serv.) Bn Royal Irish Regt
May 1917. Sheet II

Place	Date	Hour	Summary of Events and Information	Remarks and references to Appendices
ALQUINES	26th		Last day of the Training. The Divisional Staff & several of the Battalion & Company Commanders arrived to watch this training. Pte KENNY & Pte KENNY (A) did a wait. Surgeon.	
"	27th		Pte KENNY identified as the subject & daughter & attached to [illegible] men in peninsula. Services in the afternoon unsatisfactory.	
"	28th		All Companies preparing for the march, also Sports. Duty (L) 2 LO.R.E. returned Sports for LEINSTER Regt from the march, with great zest.	
WIZERNES	29th		Marched to WIZERNES that morning, arriving 15 miles to [illegible]. Cold day. Men in excellent training order. 2 Br. Harshman ([illegible]).	
STAPLES	30th		Marched to STAPLES. Second (G.T.) the march.	
CLARE CAMP	31st		Marched to CLARE CAMP. Arrived H.Q. White Brigade in the army. 2/Lt Dunne attached to H.Q. for the march. 9.3/10 P.O.W. Field Below distance 9 N.S. Officers on a route been out in an aeroplane, who District. Officers and men watched the Below shelling the aerodrome, and coming away during the night.	

E. J. Peter Bell
Lieut. Colonel.
Comd'g 8th (Serv.) Bn The Royal Irish Regt.

WAR DIARY.

FOR MONTH OF JUNE, 1917.

VOLUME:- 19

UNIT:- 6th Btn Royal Irish Regiment

SECRET

WAR DIARY of 6/7th Royal Scots Regt

INTELLIGENCE SUMMARY

Army Form C. 2118

June 1917

Place	Date	Hour	Summary of Events and Information	Remarks and references to Appendices
CLARE CAMP	1st		Quiet day cleaning up & preparing to leaving camp. Hostile aeroplane again active during the night.	
RENMORE LINES	2nd		Bn moved up to RENMORE LINES. 10 O.R. wounded on working party by enemy shells in a week's work.	
"	3rd		2/4 JONES & 25 O.R. return from an Engr construction work. Enemy bombarded & retaliated all day.	
"	4th		1 O.R. killed on working party ad CHINESE WALL. Conference ad B.H.Q. arranged for C.O.'s. Bombardment continuing.	
"	5th		Headquarters of A & D Coy move into right subsection. Bn H.Q. ad S.P.12. Relief not complete until 4 a.m. on 6th. Enemy aware of gas shells on its way up. as an inferred C & D Coys remain at RENMORE was up.	
"	6th		Hostile aeroplane up ad dawn, very low & fired all along our subline & front trenches, none of ours up. Had some C & D Coys move up to the line again. Bn 1 Offr. & 51 O.R. to (shelter B) were into support positions.	
MP SUPPORT	7th		The battle of WYSCHAETE opens ad 3:10 a.m. 12 mines going up under the German front line trench, (the map shows the whole plan). A complete success from our occupied the Ridge & became of the General Post & was carried through by any ____ as O'BRIEN BUTLER GLASS HALL O'CONNOR HUNTER FOYLE EXIT FOLK ____ of ____ & ____ & ____ ad RED ALUE LINES ad ordered ____ come the ____ camp when the ____	

HEWITT "killed MAJOR REDMOND died of wounds

SECRET

WAR DIARY or INTELLIGENCE SUMMARY

Army Form C. 2118

2nd Bn. 2(S) 12 TR Royal East Regt
Sheet 2
June 1917

Place	Date	Hour	Summary of Events and Information	Remarks and references to Appendices
PETIT BOIS	7th		at 6 p.m. held our trenches overlooked by 7th LEINSTERS & our Headquarters to concrete dugout in N.E. corner of PETIT BOIS. S.O.S. signal sent up at 11 p.m. Nothing happened. Artillery kept keeping up all night. Guns came up apparently & did considerably well as usual the whole time.	25.
ROSSIGNOL WOOD	8th		Relieved by 7th R. I. RIFLES & our Hd Qrs at ROSSIGNOL WOOD. 9.2" guns were very disturbing & to escort into wood finished day. The morning of 9th Germans were comfortable. (DEACON THOMAS) attd 6 p.m. with 20 PHILIP GIBBS) Germans gunners attached about 6 p.m. with 20 nuits. MAJOR REDMOND buried at KEMMEL	4.
RENMORE CAMP	9th		CAPT O-BRIEN-BUTLER & 2/LT WALL & 2/O.R.s buried at LOCRE. Bn moved to RENMORE LINES. Bn cinema bythographed going into Canteen. Floods newest gun still often found nearby at RENMEL with the other Floods newest gun still often found nearby at RENMEL with the other 2/LTS. HEWITT's lost found & buried near by at RENMEL with the other 2 crews.	4.
"	10th		Heavy bombardment during evening. All over.	3.
"	11th		Stand to from 6.a.m. to 6.a.m. 12th	15.
"	12th		PTE BLONDEL on 10 days leave.	
"	13th		Adjt. on leave (10 days) A2. (4 Div.) moves to MERRIS AREA.	13.

SECRET

WAR DIARY or **INTELLIGENCE SUMMARY** Army Form C. 2118

(Erase heading not required.)

of the 2/4/3/62 The Royal East Reg [illegible] Sheet 3.

June 1917

Instructions regarding War Diaries and Intelligence Summaries are contained in F.S. Regs., Part II. and the Staff Manual respectively. Title Pages will be prepared in manuscript.

Place	Date	Hour	Summary of Events and Information	Remarks and references to Appendices
MERRIS AREA	13th		2/4t KING reforms from Fauquay (IX Corps)	[illegible]
" "	14th		Entrance having commenced Rushing of O.R.s & officers commenced	[illegible]
" "	15th		Sgt. DIED to ENGLAND for commission. Sgt. MILBORN got the Croix de Guerre (2 mohs). Training all day.	[illegible]
" "	16th		Draft of C.O.R. from 2/4t KING to IV Corps School.	[illegible]
" "	17th		Colonel k.addrem 19th DIV of men offices with Runners (names) in KEMMEL SHELTERS. C.O. & by Cmdr. 20 cenrade were driven. Policy cancelled this evening. Very bad weather still.	[illegible]
" "	18th		Maur Eacl h. MERRIS and 2/4t PEMBERTON reforms. 2/t N.O.S.E from here to outlying room hyr.	[illegible]
EECKE	19th		Road to EECKE & camps ther for the night. Our find convoy arrived.	[illegible]
" "	20th		Remain at EECKE for our days cont. Army Cmdr ches ZOE come to [illegible]	[illegible]
POLLEZEELE	21st		Move to POLLEZEELE AREA, good billets for the men, very poor for officers.	[illegible]

1875 Wt. W593/826 1,000,000 4/15 J.B.C. & A. A.D.S.S./Forms/C. 2118.

Army Form C. 2118

WAR DIARY
or
INTELLIGENCE SUMMARY
(Erase heading not required.)

Instructions regarding War Diaries and Intelligence Summaries are contained in F. S. Regs., Part II. and the Staff Manual respectively. Title Pages will be prepared in manuscript.

Place	Date	Hour	Summary of Events and Information	Remarks and references to Appendices
BOLLEZEELE	23rd		LT. BRERETON 2/LTS. M. MAHON & McGOEY (both E.R.) join for duty. 2/LT. MARTIN reports. attached VIII Corps (Rumps)	F.
"	24th		Church parade at 9.30 a.m. Rogers reports from leave	F.
"	25th		Wrote of 7 o'c conv. To 10 days spend on latrinery for XIV Corps (our proper army) 2nd Lt Gt ROCHE-KELLY off on leave 10 days	F.
"	26th		Capt. Pain. Hopemans Lt. Gt ROCHE-KELLY off on leave 10 days. 2/LT SMYTH joins for duty. Am marched hard my role of Inspection by Fred. WATTS an excellent display of drill. Same two gave an excellent display of drill.	F.
"	27th		Commence hitching a rifle-ringye; 12 work-meral	F.
"	28th		30. R. joins for duty. Bad weather now raw	F.
"	29th		LT. JACKSON for duty joins today. The Docks, LT BRIDGES & 2/LT KING reports from leave & came thy had walked	F.
"	30th		This ends the Diary for month of June 1917.	F.

J. Nicholson
O'md'g 6th. (Ser.) Bn. The Royal Irish Regt.

WAR DIARY.

FOR MONTH OF JULY, 1917.

VOLUME :- 20

UNIT :- 6th R. Irish Regiment.

SECRET

Army Form C. 2118

WAR DIARY of 6/(5)(S) O.S. Th Royal Irish Regt

INTELLIGENCE SUMMARY

Sheet I

July 1917

Place	Date	Hour	Summary of Events and Information	Remarks and references to Appendices
BOLLEZEELE AREA	1		The Battalion to be inspected by the G.O.C. XIX Corps lunch on the 4th Instant. Officers on leave. Experimented with the Training of Equipment (WEBB) with grass cutter.	A
"	2		Commenced critical on B's Headquarters Field. Four (4) officers of the battalion 1st R.M.F. had rifle shoots at 200-600 yds capees.	B
"	3rd		Musketry range completed. A very extensive piece of work. An excellent job. Experts the setting of men than placed with the range. Ranges of 700 yards (a new run). Shoots of 7 & 2nd LEINSTERS.	P.
"	4th		The B's inspected by General Hickie who moved excluding General. Several so say - 10,000 classes in C Emphases of Training & M.O. Staff. Speech to all officers by Genl HICKIE. The 2nd Royal Irish the range & seen in course.	L
"	5th		Cricket match against the 47 D.O.b. The B's lost by 40 runs. A great team but lens of piece.	C
"	6th		Demonstration by ½ Section of Tanks, 27 (? Reg.) HODGE (late R. Eqns.)	B

WAR DIARY

Army Form C. 2118

of 6 H(S) B? Th. Royal Scots Bn
Sheet 2

INTELLIGENCE SUMMARY

July 1917

(Erase heading not required.)

Place	Date	Hour	Summary of Events and Information	Remarks and references to Appendices
BOLLEZEELE Area.	7th	—	Major HUTCHESON to THEGUES to train thoroughbred horses. B 49 & D Cos. cricket match against 111th Fd A. We won easily. B 6 wickets had any good match. The C.O. coming to shew them, our new good arm rest on LONDON.	
"	8th		Church parade for C of E. cancelled owing to inclement weather.	
"	9th		D Coy & 3 Ghs. 7 60 O.R. (all ranks) from no 6 all a bad draft.	
"	10th		Lt. HODGES to War Conference B. C.O. expects new draft. Cricket match against 47th Fd Ct. We won again in second innings (he a 128)	
"	11th		C.O. expects new draft (P.S.) Lieut Matron (O.S.) on the D.J. for the firearms confiscated arrived near new headquarters and so the new eight.	

SECRET

Instructions regarding War Diaries and Intelligence Summaries are contained in F. S. Regs., Part II. and the Staff Manual respectively. Title Pages will be prepared in manuscript.

Army Form C. 2118

WAR DIARY of 2/4 (S) Bn The Royal Scots Regt

Sheet 3.

INTELLIGENCE SUMMARY

(Erase heading not required.)

Month July 1917

Place	Date	Hour	Summary of Events and Information	Remarks and references to Appendices
BOLLEZEELE Area.	12th		The 4½ D. of Sports. We won 5 1st places and several 2nds & 3rds	18.
"	13th		The General held a competition for best guard of platoon. The R.I. won guard by 1 point from C.R. & my guard 3rd place in platoon competition which was won by E. Coy. C.R.	18.
"	15th		Movement orders arrive, we leave tomorrow 2/27. Crowe goes off to Brancepeth	18.
TILQUES Training area.	16th		Move to LEULINES & ETREHEM, but with considerable hostility from civilian inhabitants of Bayenghem area. The latter is a poor effort.	18.
"	17th		Runners for the B.C. on TILQUES ranges (very good ones) Competition for the best company (500x slow deliberate & rapid.) D.G. Being C.O. 2nd	18.
"	18th		Backer to attend on our training ground. Reader my Cadre.	18.
"	19th		1st day of B.C. Training	18.
"	20th		2nd ditto. General Hickie is pleased & makes a speech, and embraced	18.

WAR DIARY

INTELLIGENCE SUMMARY

of 6/2(S) B? The Royal Fus. Regt. Page 4

July 1917.

Army Form C. 2118

Place	Date	Hour	Summary of Events and Information	Remarks and references to Appendices
TILQUES Training area.	21st		Serial field day. No. of Spectators. The B. Ch. Gen. was pleased. The C.O. awarded D.S.O. & LEGION of HONOUR. 2/Lt PATMAN to M.C.	
"	23rd		Proceed to ST. OMER & entrained at 10 a.m. for ABEELE, where we arrived about 1.30 p.m. Proceed to WINNEZEELE areas by motor coach. Men fell out.	
WINNIZEELE No 2 Area			Move to WATOU No 3 Area, Marching ad 7 p.m. & arriving there about 10.30 p.m. The C.O. & both Majors on C.M. body of tomorrow at POPERINGHE.	
WATOU No 3 Area	26th		Lt. JORDAN & 6 others to recce barracks we move to YPRES.	
	30th		Move to No. 1. BRANDHOEK AREA, Marching at 7.15 a.m. arrived 10.30 p.m.	
	31st		Battle of FLANDERS commenced at 3.50 a.m. Formation handsomely all arms. Cape. cap. their final objective by the afternoon. II Corps (50am) stand to stand the counter attack at 10 p.m. very long. Ambulances from 9 p.m. to 10.15 p.m. No casualties of the battle in our ... This closes the diary for month of July 1917.	

John Ruttledge

WAR DIARY.

FOR MONTH OF AUGUST, 1917.

VOLUME 21

UNIT 6th Royal Irish Regt.

WAR DIARY
INTELLIGENCE SUMMARY

Army Form C. 2118.

5th Royal ? ? Regt
AUGUST 1917 SHEET 1.

Place	Date	Hour	Summary of Events and Information	Remarks and references to Appendices
BRANDHOEK Area No. 1.	1st		Moved at 3/2 hours notice to OLD BRITISH front line. Company ? Farm a Company up to the line.	
Up the line	2nd		Moved up into support at 2.30 am. Headquarters at RUPERT Farm. Very heavy shelling all day.	
			At 9 pm moved into front line a relieved 7 SCOTS. 2/Lt ? a Suttlehawn killed by shell. Headquarters at SOUND FARM.	
			A/Capt ? Wintle, Lieut. Sings, 2/Lt Dixon wounded a missing.	
Front line	3rd		Quiet. Shelling all day but not serious. Casualties.	
do	4th		2/Lt R.H. MARTIN wounded by a 5.9" shell a died on the day.	
do	5th		Relieved by 8th Lincolnshire Fusiliers and moved to BRANDHOEK No. 2 area. Cas'ltys for tour. Killed 7. Wounded ? 45. Missing ?	
BRANDHOEK No. 2 Area TORONTO CAMP	6th		Arrived in camp about 6 am. Bn. concentrated. B.? all ranks (?/? officers) Capt. V.E.W.H. Sumpter MC. & Bar & 2/Lt. ? on leave. 2/Lts. DUNNE & ? adjutant.	
do	7th		Battalion in rest at TORONTO CAMP	
do	8th		At rest. Company route march.	
do	9th		At rest. Company route marches.	
do	10th		? ? ? amt. 2 and 4 Other Ranks to ? ?	

ORDERLY ROOM 31 AUG 1917
5(?) Bn. The Royal (?)

WAR DIARY

INTELLIGENCE SUMMARY

Army Form C. 2118.

6th Royal Irish Regt.

AUGUST 1917. Sheet II.

Place	Date	Hour	Summary of Events and Information	Remarks and references to Appendices
SQUARE FARM front line	11th		Moved to train and marching and 6th over Front line, left attacked. Headquarters at SQUARE FARM, under about 47th Infantry Brigade. Heavy shelling on "B" Company.	
do	12th		Enemy Aeroplane very active during the morning. Heavy shelling round Headquarters. Few casualties.	
do	13th		Quiet day. Lts. adjt & S.P. in a heavy state. Comment. Lindsay fore relieved by 7th & 8th R. Innis. Fusiliers. casualties nil.	
do	14th			
do	15th		Moved on relief to VLAMERTINGHE No 3 area. Cheered on route. Remain in place. 6th Connaught Rangers. B.H.Q. at EITEL.	
VLAMERTINGHE No 3 area BIVOUAC CAMP	16th		Moved up to close support of 62nd Connaught Rangers B.H.Q. in EITEL FRITZ Trench. Came under orders of 49th Bde.	
EITEL FRITZ (Supports)	17th		Moved at about 11 p.m. on relief by 10th Sherwds. 12th Bde to VLAMERTINGHE No. 3 Area and came under 119th Bde.	
VLAMERTINGHE No 3 Area	18th		Left G.R. E. Rodi Rly. on line Aeroplane bombed the men.	
do 119 area	19th		Moved by train and marched to WATOU (B) area Lt. Bryant & details at 156 Cy. R.E. reinforcement depot. August 2/8 Killing 4 details migrated from 16th Divn.	
EECKE area	20th		Moved to EECKE area billets from STEENVOORDE.	
do	21st		Remained in above billets all day	

WAR DIARY or INTELLIGENCE SUMMARY.

Army Form C. 2118.

6th Royal Irish Regt.

AUGUST 1917

Place	Date	Hour	Summary of Events and Information	Remarks and references to Appendices
By Train & BAPAUME	22nd		Entrain at CAESTRE station at 9am. Detrain at BAPAUME at 6pm passing MARLES & ARRAS. Whilst marching to CAESTRE station got a bath in a heavy rain. On arrival in BAPAUME were quite wet, marched on arrival through wrecked town of BAPAUME to our Camp about 1½ N.E. of BAPAUME.	
Camp near GOMIECOURT & ACHIET LE GRAND	23rd		Lord Mayor's General Heavy address. Bombardt. of Russia. 2pm at CK N.5 Grand Mass intercom?	
do	24th		In Camp at Gomiecourt	
ERVILLERS	25th		Marched to Camp at ERVILLERS. (115 reinforcements here too.)	
BULLECOURT & LINE	26th		Moved into the line (Relief Complete 11.30 P.M.) relieved 16th Durham Light Infantry Bn H.Q. in Railway Cutting (called Railway Reserve) at O.25.a.5.2. night S.O.S. line just N of BULLECOURT.	
do	27th		Quiet day. Very dry weather.	
do	28th		Quiet day. weather improving. Quiet day in but shelling M/5 SMYTH on June 8.	
do	29th		Quiet day. Corps M.G. officer visited strafe. Quiet otherwise.	
do	30th		Slight artillery on our dump German propaganda dropped on lines on aerial darts.	
do	31st		Shelling "Bings" (night & together) mine (not known)	

G.N. Dolphin Major
Comdg 6th (Ser.) Bn. The Royal Irish Regt.

WAR DIARY.

FOR MONTH OF AUGUST, 1917.

VOLUME 22

UNIT 6th Royal Irish Regiment

Army Form C. 2118.

WAR DIARY
or
INTELLIGENCE SUMMARY.
(Erase heading not required.)

Sheet I 6th ROYAL IRISH REGT September 1917

Place	Date	Hour	Summary of Events and Information	Remarks and references to Appendices
Line W. of BULLECOURT	1st		Quiet day. Slight T.M. activity on right of B Coys line	
"	2nd		Enemy T.M. activity on B Coys front (night) 2 Minenwerfer took over line gun bus left on far arm left of BEAUMANS LOOP from 6th Connaught Rangers.	
"	3rd		Quiet day. Relieved by 7th Leinster Regt. at 10.30 p.m. moved out to Camp Sheet 51c B.9.a. on ST LEGER - ERVILLERS Road	
Camp near ERVILLERS.	4th		Brigadier visited camp and addressed the Battn.	
"	5th		Draft of 52 O.R. joined from 16th I.B.D. 2/Lt. Kennedy O'Neale & 2/Lt. Laughlin joined Battalion. Working parties to Brigade	
"	6th		Companys firing on 50 yds range throughout the day. 2nd Lt Roche Kelly returned from leave.	
"	7th		Coys on 50 yds. range. 2/Lt. Hamilton "Pathological" joined.	
"	8th		Battle practice by Coys. "Test attack" practiced at 10.9 p.m. + " by in parade in battle order ready to move off at 10.31 p.m.	
"	9th		Church parade in ERVILLERS in morning. Gas alarm about 10.30 p.m. Baudha floated too. Turned out to be smoke cloud & fire shell bombardment on Brigade on left & in our front	
"	10th		Battalion Drill morning parade. Working parties afternoon	
"	11th		Battalion Drill in morning.	
"	12th		Companys on rifle range during day	

Army Form C. 2118.

WAR DIARY
or
INTELLIGENCE SUMMARY.
(Erase heading not required.)

SHEET 2

6th Royal Irish Regt
September 1917

Instructions regarding War Diaries and Intelligence Summaries are contained in F. S. Regs., Part II. and the Staff Manual respectively. Title pages will be prepared in manuscript.

Place	Date	Hour	Summary of Events and Information	Remarks and references to Appendices
Camp near ERVILLERS	13th		Range firing. Practised moving to assembly position by night. Time taken &c &c	
	14th		Bn parade. Inspection etc	
line West of BULLECOURT	15th		Relieved 1st Royal Munster Fus. in front line	(3)
"	16th		Quiet morning. slight T.M. activity, no damage done	(3)
"	17th		Strafe by our artillery & T.Ms. good results. slight retaliation on our communication trench	(3)
"	18th		Quiet day	(3)
"	19th		Minor patrol encounter, one enemy hit. Our artillery active.	(3)
"	20th		Quiet morning. strafe by our artillery in afternoon, good results. Normal	(3)
"	21st		Quiet all day. 2/Lt Abercrombie Joined	(3)
"	22nd	8.50pm	Right company front heavily shelled during raid at Bn on our right, no damage done to us.	(3)
"	23rd		Quiet day. Relieved by 6th Connaught Rangers, moved into support in RAILWAY RESERVE.	(3)
In support Rly Reserve	24th to 30th		Battalion in support in RAILWAY RES. Men employed in working parties on line during this period. No operations of importance to record	(3)

E J [signature]
[signature]
6/ Royal Irish Regt

WAR DIARY

FOR MONTH OF OCTOBER, 1917.

UNIT 6th Royal Irish Regiment

VOLUME NUMBER 23

Army Form C. 2118.

6th Royal Irish Regt.
October 1917

WAR DIARY
or
INTELLIGENCE SUMMARY.
(Erase heading not required.)

Instructions regarding War Diaries and Intelligence Summaries are contained in F. S. Regs., Part II. and the Staff Manual respectively. Title pages will be prepared in manuscript.

Place	Date	Hour	Summary of Events and Information	Remarks and references to Appendices
Bullecourt Line	1st		Relieved by 1st Royal Munster Fusiliers, and moved to camp near ERVILLERS.	JMR
ERVILLERS	2nd		Attack Practice and routine of training.	JMR
	3rd		Major Hutcheson, Capt. Rutherford, Capt. Dunne on leave. G.O.C. Division presented medal ribbons in Camp.	JMR
	4th		2 Lt. McGeogh on leave.	JMR
	5th		"A" + "B" Coys on Range. Remainder of Batt. Battle Practice & Company Drill.	JMR
	6th		Companies on Rifle Range. Rapid wiring practiced.	JMR
	7th (Sunday)		Church Parade. Capt. Bridge on Leave.	JMR
	8th		Rifle Range. Drill.	JMR
	9th		Rifle Range. Wiring.	JMR
	10th		Work on DURROW CAMP.	JMR
	11th		do. Capt. Slater on Leave.	JMR
	12th		do. 2 Lt. Marten from Leave.	JMR
	13th		Bathing Parades. 2 Lt. McMahon from Leave.	JMR
	14th	"	Church Parade. Lt. Brereton from leave.	JMR
	15th		Work on DURROW CAMP.	JMR

Army Form C. 2118.

6th Royal Irish Regt.
October, 1917

WAR DIARY
or
INTELLIGENCE SUMMARY.
(Erase heading not required.)

Place	Date	Hour	Summary of Events and Information	Remarks and references to Appendices
ERVILLERS.	16th		Work in DURROW CAMP.	
BULLECOURT	17th		Relieved 1st Royal Munster Fusiliers on Brigade Front. Relief complete 9.15 p.m.	
LINE.	18th		Bde. front devided into two subsections. 6 R.I. troops over left subsection, (with Pioneer pt.) exchanged H.Q. with 6th Connaught Rangers. 'D' Coy took over Batt: Front: 'A' in Support.	
	19th		Quiet day. A few Aerial Darts on our front line. Two 4.2s on CRUX CIRCUS (Batn H.Q.) at 8.45 p.m.	
	20th		Nothing of note. 'B' & 'C' Coys to Front & Support lines respectively. 'A' & 'D' to RAILWAY RESERVE.	
	21st		Great hostile T.M. activity. Front Line & KNUCKLE LANE bombarded.	
	22nd		Quiet day. Enemy appeared very nervous.	
	23rd		At morning "Stand to" a few Aerial Darts fell in BEAUMANS LOOP. Capt. Slater from Leave.	
	24th		Enemy active all day. 5.9s & H.T.Ms intermittently on our front & support lines. 'A' Coy to front line, 'D' to Support and 'B' & 'C' to RAILWAY RESERVE.	
	25th		Very quiet day.	
	26th		Enemy gassed by our 4" Stokes at 10 p.m. Good cloud former & fairly large enemy casualties anticipated. Practically no retaliation. Two German prisoners caught from AMIENS.re-captured in W. LOOP	
	27th		Enemy gassed at 3 a.m. On this occasion very heavy retaliation which lasted from 3.20 a.m. to about 4.15. 9000 shells & 4.2s on our front line.	
	28th		Very heavy retaliation to one of our programme shoots. H.T.Ms & 5.9s	

Signed J. Roche Capt.

Army Form C. 2118.

6th Royal Irish Regt
October, 1917

WAR DIARY
or
INTELLIGENCE SUMMARY.
(Erase heading not required.)

Place	Date	Hour	Summary of Events and Information	Remarks and references to Appendices
	29th		On our front line. Six casualties (2 killed) sustained. "C" Coy to front line, "B" to Support, "A" & "D" to Reserve.	JMR JMR
	30th		Very quiet day. One casualty at night from snipers bullet.	JMR
	31st		Another quiet day.	JMR
			Enemy again rather active. T.Ms & 5.9s on STRAY SUPPORT & KNUCKLE LANE	JMR

E J McAuley
Lieut.
6 Royal Irish Regt.

WAR DIARY

FOR MONTH OF NOVEMBER, 1917.

VOLUME :- 24

UNIT :- 6th R. Irish Regiment

WAR DIARY

INTELLIGENCE SUMMARY
(Erase heading not required.)

November 1917
6th Bn. The ROYAL IRISH REGT

Army Form C. 2118.

Place	Date	Hour	Summary of Events and Information	Remarks and references to Appendices
LINE. N. of BULLECOURT	1st Nov		Quiet day, very little hostile shelling.	A
"	2nd		Relieved by 1st R. Munster Fus. moved out to DURROW CAMP near MORY	A
DURROW CAMP	3rd		Capt. at disposal of Coy Comdrs. 2/Lts. STANFORD, ROBINSON, STAFFERY, FISHER all of R.D.F. joined Battn. & Company Drill. B.F. & P.T.	A
"	4th to 12th		In DURROW CAMP. General training, Drill B.F. & P.T.	A
"	13th		Relieved the 1st R Munster Fus. in left subsection. "C" Coy left at ST LEGER receiving instruction in wiring	A
"	14th		Quiet day, no hostile artillery activity	A
"	15th		Our artillery & T.Ms very active	A
"	16th		Our artillery very active wire cutting	A
"	17th		Fairly quiet, Our M.Guns active at night.	A
"	18th		Enemy artillery active. Shelled battery position behind Bn HQ during the afternoon. Relieved by 1st R. Munster Fus. & proceeded to DURROW CAMP	A
DURROW CAMP	19th		Coys. at disposal of Coy Comdrs. "Commencement of the "ACTION of CROISILLES HEIGHTS" At 6.30am 18th RMF & 6th Leim Rangers attacked & occupied TUNNEL TR. in conjunction with Divn	A
"	20th		On right & Brigade on left. The Bn. moved up to close support, & then back to DURROW CAMP in the evening remaining in Brigade Reserve. "C" Coy wiring in front of TUNNEL TR. Lieut. GRAYSON killed	A

WAR DIARY

INTELLIGENCE SUMMARY.

November 1917   Army Form C. 2118.

6th Bn. The ROYAL IRISH REGT.

(Erase heading not required.)

Place	Date	Hour	Summary of Events and Information	Remarks and references to Appendices
	Nov.			
DURROW CAMP	21st		In Brigade Reserve.	
Line Left Sub-Section. N. of BULLECOURT	22nd		Moved into line & relieved 1st R. Munster Regt. Bn. HQ in STRAY SUPPORT, 2 Coys in TUNNEL TR. and 2 Coys in close support. 'C' Coy. rejoined.	
"	23rd		Quiet day, wiring and consolidation continued.	
"	24th		do.	
"	25th		do.	
"	26th		"A" & "C" Coys moved up from support Trenches & took over right subsection from 7th Leinster Regt. Left BRIDGE.	
"	27th		Fairly quiet day. 2/Lt FISHER, wounded on patrol, small patrol encounters.	
"	28th		12 phosgene & 8 hty. trench mortar boys captured. Heavy trench barrage from 5.30 AM to 6.30 AM. Heavy hostile bombardment on our front & support lines 7 & 7.15 p.m. Little damage done on our front & support lines & C.T.s.	
"	29th		Harassing fire continued during the day. Little damage done. Our artillery retaliated effectively.	
"	30th		Heavy hostile bombardment on front, support lines & C.T. 6.25 AM & 6.50 AM. Again at 9 AM. till 10 AM & 12 noon till 1 PM. Our artillery retaliated effectively. Quiet night. Our planes bombed COPSE TR.	

1st Decr. 1917

E John D Kelly Lieut Col.

Cmdg. 6th Royal Irish Regt.

WAR DIARY,

FOR MONTH OF DECEMBER, 1917.

VOLUME :-25.

UNIT :- 6th R. Irish Regiment.

WAR DIARY
~~INTELLIGENCE SUMMARY~~

(Erase heading not required.)

6th ROYAL IRISH REGT
Army Form C. 2118.

December 1917

Place	Date	Hour	Summary of Events and Information	Remarks and references to Appendices
Trenches N.W. (BULLECOURT) (TUNNEL TR.)	Dec 1st		At 6.17 P.M. a sharp barrage was put down on our frontline (TUNNEL TR.) and QUEEN'S LANE lasting about 15 mins. Our artillery retaliated promptly.	
"	2nd		Quiet day. Relieved by 17th WELSH about 7 p.m. Moved to camp at GOMMECOURT	
On the march	3rd		Bde. marched from GOMMECOURT to BEAUVENCOURT (3 kilm. S. of BAPAUME).	
BEAUVENCOURT Hd	5th		In camp, weather very cold.	
On the march	6th		Marched to BUIRE on TINCOURT–PÉRONNE road	
BUIRE	7th to 10th		In camp at BUIRE. Cleaning up and kit inspections. Weather still cold.	
"	11th		Marched to STE EMILIE and took over from 7th Leinster Regt in Brigade Reserve. Right section Posten, in huts scattered amongst the ruins of the village, alongside Billets shelled between 6 & 9 p.m. No casualties but lost 7th R.I. Regt.	
STE EMILIE	12th		tapped heavily.	
"	13th		Bosch moved back to bivouacs in railway cutting went by STE EMILIE at west end of village on road to Rly. cutting	
"	14th to 16th		Nothing to report.	
EPÉHY Sector Right sub-section	17th		Relieved 7th Leinster Regt in frontline right subsection.	
"	18th to 20		Nothing to report. Very quiet. Weather cold and much snow on ground	
"	21st		T.M. Strafe on GILLEMONT POST about 12.30 p.m. Little damage, no casualties	

Army Form C. 2118.

WAR DIARY
or
INTELLIGENCE SUMMARY.
(Erase heading not required.)

6th ROYAL IRISH REGT.
December 1917

Place	Date	Hour	Summary of Events and Information	Remarks and references to Appendices
EPÉHY LEFT SECTION Right sub-section	22nd		Very quiet day. Some artillery fire on QUECHETTES WOOD about noon.	
"	23rd		Quiet morning. T.M. strafe on GILLEMONT POST about 5.30 P.M. and also some shelling. Z COPSE (Coy. Bn. HQ.) also shelled. Enemy attempted to raid GILLEMONT POST with about 50 men. He was driven off by our Lewis gun fire. Relieved by 2nd Royal Irish & marched out to billets in VILLERS FAUCON	
VILLERS FAUCON 24th			Cleaning up and inspections.	
"	25th		Divine service in morning. Christmas Dinner	
"	26th to 28th		Nothing to report.	
Left Section EPÉHY sub	29th		Relieved 1st Royal Dublin Fus. in Brigade support. Battalion distributed in strong points in front of KEMPIRE - EPÉHY road. HQ. in KEMPIRE. Capt PRICE M.C. Lt JACKSON, and Lieut MOVAT-BIGGS joined from D. Batt Bn.	
"	30th		Quiet day. 1/Lt BANKS took over duties of Transport Officer	
"	31st		Quiet day. Working parties supplied at night.	

Glen .... Capt
for Major
Cmdg. 6th Royal Irish Regt.

WAR DIARY,

FOR MONTH OF JANUARY, 1918.

VOLUME:- 26

UNIT:- 6th R. Irish Regiment.

WAR DIARY
INTELLIGENCE SUMMARY.
(Erase heading not required.)

Army Form C. 2118.

6th ROYAL IRISH REGT.
January 1918

Place	Date	Hour	Summary of Events and Information	Remarks and references to Appendices
EPÉHY left section	1st to 3rd		In Brigade Support. Weather very cold, situation quiet, working parties supplied	
"	4th		Relieved 7th Leinster Regt. in front line, situation quiet, left intersection.	
"	5th to 9th		Situation quiet except for some shelling on right Coy.- & on Battn. HQrs. on 7th, 8th & 9th.	
"	10th		Weather very cold with heavy snow falls.	
"	10th		Relieved by 2nd Royal Irish Regt., Battn. marched to Ste EMILIE & entrained there, proceeding by train to TINCOURT	
TINCOURT Brigade Reserve	11th & 12th		A training programme prepared and carried out by Coys. under Coy. Commanders. Range practice carried out.	
"	15th		Battn. furnished large wiring party for wiring support defences around RONSSOY	
"	16th to 18th		The Battalion supplied large wiring parties for wiring support defences by the Battn.	
"	19th		Training programme carried out. Working parties supplied by the Battn.	
"	19th		The Battn. was inspected by Brig. Gen. Griogne D.S.O. cmdg. 47th I.B.	
"	20th		First working parties supplied. Church parades during the morning	
"	21st		Battn. for the Battalion at TINCOURT. Armourers Inspection	
EPÉHY right section	22nd		The Battn. marched to Ste EMILIE relieving 8/9th Royal Dublin Fusiliers in Brigade Reserve. Right Section. Ste EMILIE heavily shelled from 3 to 4 p.m. during relief. No casualties occurred. Battn. billeted in huts in light railway cutting west of Ste EMILIE	

WAR DIARY

INTELLIGENCE SUMMARY.
(Erase heading not required.)

Army Form C. 2118.

6th ROYAL IRISH REGT
January 1916

Place	Date	Hour	Summary of Events and Information	Remarks and references to Appendices
EPÉHY Right Section	23rd		Quiet day. A few shells fell near the Railway crossing at 7pm	
"	24th & 27th		Nothing to record. No hostile shelling in neighbourhood of ST EMILIE.	
"	28th		Relieved 7th Leinster Regt in right subsection. Enemy activity quiet except for short bursts of machine gun fire at stormy period.	
"	29th		Quiet day, very good visibility. Enemy were on night work party examined by a strong patrol from B Coy. No enemy patrols encountered.	
"	30th		Quiet day, very good visibility. Test S.O.S. worked out at 4.30 A.M. & 8 P.M. An inter company relief was carried out between 6 & 7 pm.	
"	31st		Quiet day. No opportunity to reconnoitre. A heavy fog lasted through the day. A patrol went out from "D" Coy from 5pm to examine enemy wire. A hostile patrol was heard but no contact was obtained.	

1st February 1916

E. J. ashley
Lieut Col.
Comdg. 6th Bn. The Royal Irish Regt

WAR DIARY.

FOR MONTH OF FEBRUARY, 1918.

VOLUME :- 24.

UNIT :- 6th Royal Irish Regiment.

Army Form C. 2118

WAR DIARY
or
INTELLIGENCE SUMMARY.
(Erase heading not required.)

Instructions regarding War Diaries and Intelligence Summaries are contained in F.S. Regs., Part II. and the Staff Manual respectively. Title pages will be prepared in manuscript.

1918 February

Place	Date	Hour	Summary of Events and Information	Remarks and references to Appendices
	1st		Quiet day. Bad visibility. Orders for the disbandment of the Battalion received. Battn. to be divided between the 2nd R. Irish & the 7th R. Irish (S.I.H).	F.108.
LEMPIRE	2nd		Relieved by 7th Leinster Regt. Moved into support in LEMPIRE & RONSSOY. Took over billets vacated by 1st R. Munster Fusiliers.	F.108.
SAULCOURT	3rd		Relieved by 2nd Lincoln Regt. Moved to Camp at SAULCOURT.	F.108.
	4th		At SAULCOURT. Preparing for disbandment.	F.108.
	5th		do.	F.108.
	6th		do.	F.108.
	7th		do.	F.108.
	8th		do. Found Working Party 200 strong at Left Bde. H.Q.	F.108.
	9th		Battalion disbanded. At 1.30 p.m. 7 Offrs & 296 O.Rs. proceeded to HAMEL to join 2nd Royal Irish Regt. and at 2.30 p.m. 6 Offs & 313 O.Rs. proceeded to VILLERS-FAUCON to the 7th R. Irish Regt (S.I.H). H.Q. Staff & Transport Personnel remained to settle Battn. Officers were not posted to new units.	F.108.

J.M.M.Lekish
Major
Cmdg. 2nd R. Irish Regt.

www.ingramcontent.com/pod-product-compliance
Lightning Source LLC
Chambersburg PA
CBHW081429160426
43193CB00013B/2229